What People Are Saying about Threshold Bible Study

"This remarkable series provides a method of study and reflection that is bound to produce rich fruit."   Dianne Bergant, C.S.A., Catholic Theological Union, Chicago

"This fine series will provide needed tools that can deepen your understanding of Scripture, but most importantly it can deepen your faith."
          Most Reverend Charles J. Chaput, O.F.M. Cap., Archbishop of Denver

"Threshold Bible Study is a wonderful series that helps modern people read the Bible with insight and joy."   Richard J. Clifford, S.J., Weston Jesuit School of Theology

"The commentary of Stephen Binz does far more than inform; it asks for commitment and assent on the part of the reader/prayer."
          Kathleen O'Connell Chesto, author of F.I.R.E. and Why Are the Dandelions Weeds?

"This is a wonderful gift for those wishing to make a home for the Word in their hearts."
          Carol J. Dempsey, OP, Associate Professor of Theology, University of Portland, OR

"Written in a sprightly easy-to-understand style, these volumes will engage the mind, heart, and spirit."   Alexander A. Di Lella, O.F.M., The Catholic University of America

"By covering a wide variety of themes and topics, Threshold Bible Study continually breathes new life into ancient texts."   John R. Donahue, S.J., St. Mary's Seminary and University

"Threshold Bible Study successfully bridges the painful gap between solid biblical scholarship and the rich spiritual nourishment that we expect to find in the words of Scripture."
          Demetrius Dumm, O.S.B., Saint Vincent Archabbey

"Threshold Bible Study offers a marvelous new approach for individuals and groups to study themes in our rich biblical and theological tradition."
          John Endres, S.J., Jesuit School of Theology, Berkeley

"Threshold Bible Study enables Catholics to read, with greater understanding, the Bible in the Church."   Francis Cardinal George, O.M.I., Archbishop of Chicago

"Threshold Bible Study offers you an encounter with the Word that will make your heart come alive."   Tim Gray, Director of the Denver Catholic Biblical School

"Threshold Bible Study offers solid scholarship and spiritual depth."
                                        Scott Hahn, Franciscan University of Steubenville

"Threshold Bible Study offers those who want to begin faith-filled and prayerful study of the Bible with a user-friendly tool."   Leslie J. Hoppe, O.F.M., Catholic Theological Union

"Threshold Bible Study is a fine blend of the best of biblical scholarship and a realistic sensitivity to the spiritual journey of the believing Christian."
                                        Francis J. Moloney, S.D.B., The Catholic University of America

"An invaluable guide that can make reading the Bible enjoyable and truly nourishing."
                                        Jacques Nieuviarts, Institut Catholique de Toulouse

"Threshold Bible Study is a refreshing approach to enable participants to ponder the Scriptures more deeply."   Irene Nowell, O.S.B., Mount St. Scholastica

"Threshold Bible Study stands in the tradition of the biblical renewal movement and brings it back to life."   Kathleen M. O'Connor, Columbia Theological Seminary

"This series is exceptional for its scholarly solidity, pastoral practicality, and clarity of presentation."   Peter C. Phan, Georgetown University

"Threshold Bible Study is the perfect series of Bible study books for serious students with limited time."   John J. Pilch, Georgetown University

"These thematic books are informative, easy to use, rooted in the Church's tradition of reflection and prayer, and of sound catechetical method."
                                        Most Reverend Anthony M. Pilla, Bishop of Cleveland

"Threshold Bible Study is an enriching and enlightening approach to understanding the rich faith which the Scriptures hold for us today."
                                        Abbot Gregory J. Polan, O.S.B., Conception Abbey and Seminary College

"Threshold Bible Study leads the reader from Bible study to personal prayer, community involvement, and active Christian commitment in the world."
                                        Sandra M. Schneiders, Jesuit School of Theology, Berkeley

"This is the best material I have seen for serious Bible study."
                                        Most Reverend Donald W. Trautman, Bishop of Erie

"Guaranteed to make your love of Scripture grow!"
                                        Ronald D. Witherup, S.S., author of The Bible Companion

ANGELS
of GOD

Stephen J. Binz

Second printing 2009

The Scripture passages contained herein are from the *New Revised Standard Version of the Bible*, Catholic edition. Copyright ©1989, by the Division of Christian Education of the National Council of Churches in the U.S.A. All rights reserved.

TWENTY-THIRD PUBLICATIONS
A Division of Bayard
One Montauk Avenue, Suite 200
P.O. Box 6015
New London, CT 06320
(860) 437-3012 or (800) 321-0411
www.23rdpublications.com
ISBN 978-1-58595-518-3

Library of Congress Catalog Card Number: 2005929305
Printed in the U.S.A.

Contents

LESSONS 13-18

LESSONS 19-24

LESSONS 25-30

How to Use Threshold Bible Study

Each book in the Threshold Bible Study series is designed to lead you through a new doorway of biblical awareness, to accompany you across a unique threshold of understanding. The characters, places, and images that you encounter in each of these topical studies will help you explore fresh dimensions of your faith and discover richer insights for your spiritual life.

Threshold Bible Study covers biblical themes in depth in a short amount of time. Unlike more traditional Bible studies that treat a biblical book or series of books, Threshold Bible Study aims to address specific topics within the entire Bible. The goal is not for you to comprehend everything about each passage, but rather for you to understand what a variety of passages from different books of the Bible reveals about the topic of each study.

Threshold Bible Study offers you an opportunity to explore the entire Bible from the viewpoint of a variety of different themes. The commentary that follows each biblical passage launches your reflection about that passage and helps you begin to see its significance within the context of your contemporary experience. The questions following the commentary challenge you to understand the passage more fully and apply it to your own life. The prayer starter helps conclude your study by integrating learning into your relationship with God.

These studies are designed for maximum flexibility. Each study is presented in a workbook format, with sections for reading, reflecting, writing, discussing, and praying. Space for writing after each question is ideal for personal study and allows group members to prepare in advance for their discussion. The thirty lessons in each topic may be used by an individual over the period of a month, or by a group for six sessions, with lessons to be studied each week before the next group meeting. These studies are ideal for Bible study groups, small Christian communities, adult faith formation, student groups, Sunday school, neighborhood groups, and family reading, as well as for individual learning.

The method of Threshold Bible Study is rooted in the classical tradition of *lectio divina,* an ancient yet contemporary means for reading the Scriptures reflectively and prayerfully. Reading and interpreting the text (*lectio*) is followed by reflective meditation on its message (*meditatio*). This reading and reflecting flows into prayer from the heart (*oratio* and *contemplatio*).

This ancient method assures us that Bible study is a matter of both the mind and the heart. It is not just an intellectual exercise to learn more and be able to discuss the Bible with others. It is, more importantly, a transforming experience. Reflecting on God's word, guided by the Holy Spirit, illumines the mind with wisdom and stirs the heart with zeal.

Following the personal Bible study, Threshold Bible Study offers a method for extending *lectio divina* into a weekly conversation with a small group. This communal experience will allow participants to enhance their appreciation of the message and build up a spiritual community (*collatio*). The end result will be to increase not only individual faith, but also faithful witness in the context of daily life (*operatio*).

Through the spiritual disciplines of Scripture reading, study, reflection, conversation, and prayer, you will experience God's grace more abundantly as your life is rooted more deeply in Christ. The risen Jesus said: "Listen! I am standing at the door, knocking; if you hear my voice and open the door, I will come in to you and eat with you, and you with me" (Rev 3:20). Listen to the Word of God, open the door, and cross the threshold to an unimaginable dwelling with God!

SUGGESTIONS FOR INDIVIDUAL STUDY

• Make your Bible reading a time of prayer. Ask for God's guidance as your read the Scriptures.

• Try to study daily, or as often as possible according to the circumstances of your life.

• Read the Bible passage carefully, trying to understand both its meaning and its personal application as you read. Some find it helpful to read the passage aloud.

• Read the passage in another Bible translation. Each version adds to your understanding of the original text.

• Allow the commentary to help you comprehend and apply the scriptural text. The commentary is only a beginning, not the last word on the meaning of the passage.

• After reflecting on each question, write out your response. The very act of writing will help you clarify your thoughts, bring new insights, and amplify your understanding.

• As you reflect on your answers, think about how you can live God's word in the context of your daily life.

• Conclude each daily lesson by reading the prayer and continuing with your own prayer from the heart.

• Make sure your reflections and prayers are matters of both the mind and the heart. A true encounter with God's word is always a transforming experience.

• Choose a word or a phrase from the lesson to carry with you throughout the day as a reminder of your encounter with God's life-changing word.

• Share your learning experience with at least one other person whom you trust for additional insights and affirmation. The ideal way to share learning is in a small group that meets regularly.

SUGGESTIONS FOR GROUP STUDY

• Meet regularly; weekly is ideal. Try to be on time and make attendance a high priority for the sake of the group. The average group meets for about an hour.

• Open each session with a prepared prayer, a song, or a reflection. Find some appropriate way to bring the group from the workaday world into a sacred time of graced sharing.

• If you have not been together before, name tags are very helpful as a group begins to become acquainted with the other group members.

• Spend the first session getting acquainted with one another, reading the Introduction aloud, and discussing the questions that follow.

• Appoint a group facilitator to guide the discussion. The role of facilitator may rotate among members each week. The facilitator simply keeps the discussion on track; each person shares responsibility for the group. There is no need for the facilitator to be a trained teacher.

• Try to study the six lessons on your own during the week. When you have done your own reflection and written your own answers, you will be better prepared to discuss the six scriptural lessons with the group. If you have not had an opportunity to study the passages during the week, meet with the group anyway to share support and insights.

• Participate in the discussion as much as you are able, offering your thoughts, insights, feelings, and decisions. You learn by sharing with others the fruits of your study.

• Be careful not to dominate the discussion. It is important that everyone in the group be offered an equal opportunity to share the results of their work. Try to link what you say to the comments of others so that the group remains on the topic.

• When discussing your own personal thoughts or feelings, use "I" language. Be as personal and honest as appropriate and be very cautious about giving advice to others.

• Listen attentively to the other members of the group so as to learn from their insights. The words of the Bible affect each person in a different way, so a group provides a wealth of understanding for each member.

• Don't fear silence. Silence in a group is as important as silence in personal study. It allows individuals time to listen to the voice of God's Spirit and the opportunity to form their thoughts before they speak.

• Solicit several responses for each question. The thoughts of different people will build on the answers of others and will lead to deeper insights for all.

• Don't fear controversy. Differences of opinions are a sign of a healthy and honest group. If you cannot resolve an issue, continue on, agreeing to disagree. There is probably some truth in each viewpoint.

• Discuss the questions that seem most important for the group. There is no need to cover all the questions in the group session.

• Realize that some questions about the Bible cannot be resolved, even by experts. Don't get stuck on some issue for which there are no clear answers.

• Whatever is said in the group is said in confidence and should be regarded as such.

• Pray as a group in whatever way feels comfortable. Pray for the members of your group throughout the week.

Schedule for group study

Session 1: Introduction   Date: _____

Session 2: Lessons 1-6   Date: _____

Session 3: Lessons 7-12   Date: _____

Session 4: Lessons 13-18   Date: _____

Session 5: Lessons 19-24   Date: _____

Session 6: Lessons 25-30   Date: _____

He will command his angels concerning you, to guard you in all your ways.
Ps 91:11

Angels Of God

S cience tells us that our eyes can only see a small slice of the total reality that is around us. Visible light is just one band of wavelengths in the electromagnetic spectrum. Other electromagnetic waves, such as gamma rays, X rays, and radio waves are no different from light except that our eyes cannot detect them. If our eyes were sensitive to the wavelength our microwave oven used, we wouldn't need a light bulb inside to see what's cooking! The proverbial phrase, "there is more than meets the eye," is a truth about the fullness of reality. Similarly, there are more sounds in the world than can be detected with the human ear. Other living creatures can hear sounds that are above or below the pitches our ears can hear and electronic listening devises inform us that there is an enormous range of sound that fills the universe. Because of scientific discoveries, we know much more about the world than our five senses can tell us.

Likewise, because of God's revelation, we know more about reality than we could discover on our own. The revelation of God tells us that God's creation includes not only the physical earth and its living creatures, but also a whole world of invisible creation. In faith we know that God created the heavens and the earth, things that are seen and unseen. The world is filled not only with material creation, but also the invisible reality of angels. We cannot hear all the sounds that fill our world, yet the message and song of the angels fill the universe. We cannot see all the reality that fills our world, but we know

1

that we are surrounded by ministering spirits who have been sent forth to serve God (Heb 1:14).

When angels appear in the biblical stories, it is usually at the point of deepest mystery, when the wonder of God touches the lives of people most profoundly. They take us into the most dramatic scenes of the Old and New Testament. Like a spotlight shining on stage at the key moments, the appearances of the angels highlight the meaning and magnificence of God's action among his people.

Reflection and discussion

• Why is it difficult for me to believe more than what I can perceive with my five senses? What indicates to me that there is more in the world than what meets the eye?

• What do I already know about angels? What do I hope to learn?

Ministers of the Living God

The angels in the Bible are most identified by their mission rather than their form. Both the Hebrew word for angel (*mal'ak*) and the Greek word (*angelos*) mean "messenger." The word in itself says nothing about the essence or the form of these created beings. The biblical narratives rarely describe an angel's appearance; rather, they describe an angel's effect on people and on events. In many biblical texts, the angel of God seems almost equivalent to God, a manifestation of God's saving will and concern in earthly life.

Though the angels are only occasionally manifested in human experience, they are a constant presence. The appearances of the angels are always in keeping with their function in the account, symbolic expressions of their ever-present activity. They mediate the power, support, and deliverance of God to human beings. They sometimes become visible in the biblical narratives so that certain people may benefit from the recognition of their presence. They speak in God's voice, become known as a mysterious presence, appear as fire and light, become visible in the form of human beings, or move through the air and encounter people on the earth. Yet a special kind of sight is necessary for angels to become visible, a sight which comes as a gift from God. When angels appear in the world, their presence reveals their spiritual world as integral to ours. They invite those who see them to step over the boundaries and limitations of the material world to recognize its share in the boundless and unlimited world of spiritual beings.

As presented in the Bible, the angels always call attention to God and to God's will for humanity. They point beyond themselves to the one who sends them. They never do anything on their own, but only what God wants and assigns them to do. Like the moon, they do not shine their own light; those who see them are always aware of the greater light they reflect. In relationship to humanity, the angels serve as mediators, messengers, guardians, and guides.

All the activity of angels is relational. The angels function within the embrace of God's care for creation and within the network of that mutual help, guidance, and intercession that ideally characterizes the relationships of people with one another. Their primary activity is to do God's will in loving obedience. The angels are either turned toward God in worship and praise, or toward human beings as bearers of God's revelation, providence, and protection.

Contrary to popular thought today, the appearance of an angel is not an event marked by sentimental sweetness and happiness. The biblical characters always demonstrated a respectful fear when an angel appeared. They knew that angels did not come to make life more serene, cheerful, and contented; usually they turned life upside-down. The angels always do more than simply manifest their presence. They demonstrate God's power and often point people's lives in a different direction.

Reflection and discussion

• Why does God occasionally manifest the presence of angels in the world of human experience? Of what benefit are the angels to those who experience them?

• In what way are the angels' appearances to people in the Bible different from their popular characterization today?

The Mission of God's Angels

Among the many functions of the angels in the Israelite and Christian traditions, their role as intermediaries is crucial. They are constantly crossing the divide between God and humanity, bridging the gulf between heaven and earth. Because they are in direct touch with God, angels reveal God in their very essence. They help people on earth to perceive divine power in the world, and prepare them for ever-deeper experiences of God and ultimately for union with God.

There was a strong conviction in ancient Israel that human beings were not capable of having an unmediated encounter with God. Expressing the dangers of a divine encounter, God said to Moses, "You cannot see my face; for no one shall see me and live" (Exod 33:20). So encounters between God and human beings in the Bible often involve the mediation of angels. Through angels, God is present, though not directly. The fiery angel speaking to Moses from the bush joined the divine world to the material earth. God's voice is heard, his power is felt, his presence is real, but in a way that our humanity can begin to comprehend.

The ladder envisioned by Jacob, the stairway connecting heaven and earth with angels ascending and descending, symbolizes the Old Testament mediation of angels. They bring the saving power of God to humanity and invite individuals to step over the boundaries of the material world into the limitless world of God. In the world of ancient Israel, the fiery seraphim and cherubim were known as guardian figures of God's heavenly throne, preventing full access to God's presence, hiding God's glory with their protective wings. Yet, in the New Testament the angels' mediation is overshadowed by the perfect mediation of Jesus Christ. As both divine and human, his very being is the presence of God in the world and the perfect expression of humanity joined to God. Superior to the angels and adored by them, Christ breaks the boundaries that prevent access to God and opens wide the passage to heaven. As sharers in the mediation of Christ, the angels serve him and facilitate God's mission of bringing salvation to all people through him.

Closely united with the angels' function as intermediaries is their role as messengers of God. The angels never speak or act simply on their own; they always speak for and act on behalf of God. Yet, as messengers, they are not mere couriers. They are more like representatives or ambassadors who speak and act in the place of the one who sent them. As bearers of God's word and will, the angelic messengers appear at strategic points in the history of salvation. Often their message is in the form of a birth announcement, heralding new possibility into the lives of people who had begun to lose hope. At other times their message is a commission to lead God's people. The angel comes not only to communicate a message but also to offer tangible assurance that God is continually present with the one he calls. At still other times the angels announce divine help to God's people and offer instructions that move God's saving plan to a new stage in history.

A further aspect of the mission of God's angels is their service as guardians of God's people. The Israelites experienced the protective care of God on their perilous trek through the wilderness and in the establishment of their place as a nation in the promised land. But they also experienced God's personal and individual care as shown in the angels' protection of Hagar and Ishmael in the desert, of Isaac in the testing of Abraham on the mountain, of the three young men in the fiery furnace of Babylon and Daniel in the lion's den, of Tobias along his journey, and of Peter in his prison cell.

The Bible offers credible evidence of individual guardian angels for each person, offering not a substitute for God's loving presence, but a manifestation of it. Like God, the angels care about each individual person. As Jesus tells us, "There is joy in the presence of the angels of God over one sinner who repents" (Luke 15:10). Jesus urges us to take care of God's lowly people, "for I tell you, in heaven their angels continually see the face of my Father in heaven" (Matt 18:10). The personal ministry of guardian angels is an extension of God's unbroken attention toward us: guiding us, protecting us, rescuing us, and ultimately bringing us to everlasting life. The God who is so intimately involved even with the flowers and birds that not a single sparrow falls to earth without the Father's knowledge also helps each individual person through the ministry of his angels.

But even though we experience intimacy with God through the mission of his angels, we cannot tell the good news of angels without also admitting the bad news. Though created by God as good in their nature, angels were given a will to choose how they would respond to their Creator. Some chose to reject God and his reign, becoming adversaries of God's kingdom. Those who chose to rebel became adversaries of God's saving will for humanity and spend their angelic energies tempting humanity to reject God's loving plan. Though Jesus spent his ministry breaking the powers of evil in the world and freeing people from demonic bondage, even Jesus was tempted by the devil. His saving death and resurrection conquered the powers of Satan, but the final implementation of that victory awaits Christ's glorious coming at the end of time. Meanwhile we struggle with a deceptive enemy, disguised as an angel of light (2 Cor 11:14), prowling like a lion (1 Pet 5:8). Yet we remain steadfast in faith and joyful in hope, knowing that the war is won though the struggle continues. The power of evil is defeated; the influence of Satan is limited and his days are numbered (Rev 12:12).

Though some angels have rebelled, the vast majority of God's angels will accompany Christ at his glorious coming. They function as ministers of God's judgment, working to bring about the final triumph of God over evil and bringing creation to completion. All the angels will accompany Jesus as he comes as judge of the living and the dead, and they will gather the faithful into God's eternal kingdom (Matthew 24:31; 25:31). In the book of

Revelation, angels fill the visions, interpreting God's final will for humanity and guiding the progress of events leading up to the completion of God's creation in the new and eternal Jerusalem.

The highest service of God performed by the angels is worship. If we were to hear it unimpeded, the song of the angels would surely be a most beautiful sound. In their eternal praise of God, their ministry finds its origin and its purpose. The worship of the Church on earth is a participation in the worship offered by the angels in heaven. When we worship we are offered the continual assistance of the angels, helping us bring our worship more in tune with theirs. Only when the effects of sin are purified from our lives in God's eternity will we be able to fully share the music of the angels and worship God with perfect love and in harmony with all creation.

Reflection and discussion

• Which of the many functions of the angels in the Bible seems the most important to me?

• Which of the functions of God's angels surprises me? What angelic mission do I want to learn more about?

The Angels and Us

Whenever I travel to New York from the small city in which I live, I am always a bit awed by the masses of people coming at me on the sidewalks, traveling in all directions. Then I think about all the people living and working above me in the massive skyscrapers and all the people traveling below me in the subways. My mind expands to the planes flying above from places throughout the world and the web of connections of these fellow human beings with the masses of people in other places across the globe. Trying to imagine that God sustains the lives of each of these people and cares for them individually, not just now but throughout their lifespan and into eternal life, is a bit too much for my mind to comprehend.

But this study of God's angels has given me a new way to think about God's providential care for each individual person. God's myriad of angels makes his promise, "I will never leave you or forsake you" (Heb 13:5), seem real and possible. Having God's angels as intermediaries, messengers, and guardians gives me confidence to sing with the psalmist: "For he will command his angels concerning you, to guard you in all your ways. On their hands they will bear you up, so that you do not dash your foot against a stone" (Ps 91:11–12).

If angels are created spiritual beings, then they can come to us through their own spiritual power, through other people, in our dreams and imaginations, in sudden insights that flash through our minds. They come to help us interpret life and to help us in healing and guiding ways. In these many ways, angels make God's loving closeness tangible, expressed in real experiences. They connect our world with the world of God. Angels are one way in which the unfathomable mystery of God enters into our everyday reality.

The more we study the work of God's angels within the history of salvation, the more we may become aware of their presence here and now: in our personal lives, in works of generosity and care for others, in God's ongoing revelation of himself to us, and in the liturgical worship of the Church on earth. Greater awareness and deeper understanding of the mediation and ministry of angels will help us be more aware of the full potential of our relationship with God.

Reflection and discussion

• How might the angels help me to trust more confidently in God's providential care?

• What divides our world from the spiritual world of God's heavenly agents? In what way can the loving ministry of the angels better connect our world with God's world?

Prayer

Creator God, you have made all things, both material and spiritual. Thank you for the mission of your angels as mediators, messengers, guardians, and ministers of your justice and loving care. During this study, teach me the many ways that you manifest your saving love to me and help me to understand more clearly the mystery of your devoted providence. Send your angels to minister your will for me and to guide, encourage, and enlighten me as I read and contemplate your inspired word.

SUGGESTIONS FOR FACILITATORS, GROUP SESSION 1

1. If the group is meeting for the first time, or if there are newcomers joining the group, it is helpful to provide nametags.

2. Distribute the books to the members of the group.

3. You may want to ask the participants to introduce themselves and tell the group a bit about themselves.

4. Ask one or more of these introductory questions:
   - What drew you to join this group?
   - What is your biggest fear in beginning this Bible study?
   - How is beginning this study like a "threshold" for you?

5. You may want to pray this prayer as a group:

Come upon us, Holy Spirit, to enlighten and guide us as we begin this study of God's angels. You inspired the biblical authors to express the marvels of the angels in God's plan to save his people. Now stir our minds and our hearts to penetrate the wonders of the angels and allow them to manifest their presence in our lives. Motivate us to read the Scriptures and give us a deeper love for God's word each day. Bless us during this session and throughout the coming week with the fire of your love.

6. Read the Introduction aloud, pausing at each question for discussion. Group members may wish to write the insights of the group as each question is discussed. Encourage several members of the group to respond to each question.

7. Don't feel compelled to finish the complete Introduction during the session. It is better to allow sufficient time to talk about the questions raised than to rush to the end. Group members may read any remaining sections on their own after the group meeting.

8. Instruct group members to read the first six lessons on their own during the six days before the next group meeting. They should write out their own answers to the questions as preparation for next week's group discussion.

9. Fill in the date for each group meeting under "Schedule for Group Study."

10. Conclude by praying aloud together the prayer at the end of the Introduction.

Jacob dreamed that there was a ladder set up on the earth, the top of it reaching to heaven; and the angels of God were ascending and descending on it. Gen 28:12

Stairway to Heaven

GENESIS 28:10–22 ¹⁰*Jacob left Beer-sheba and went toward Haran.* ¹¹*He came to a certain place and stayed there for the night, because the sun had set. Taking one of the stones of the place, he put it under his head and lay down in that place.* ¹²*And he dreamed that there was a ladder set up on the earth, the top of it reaching to heaven; and the angels of God were ascending and descending on it.* ¹³*And the Lord stood beside him and said, "I am the Lord, the God of Abraham your father and the God of Isaac; the land on which you lie I will give to you and to your offspring;* ¹⁴*and your offspring shall be like the dust of the earth, and you shall spread abroad to the west and to the east and to the north and to the south; and all the families of the earth shall be blessed in you and in your offspring.* ¹⁵*Know that I am with you and will keep you wherever you go, and will bring you back to this land; for I will not leave you until I have done what I have promised you."*

¹⁶*Then Jacob woke from his sleep and said, "Surely the Lord is in this place— and I did not know it!"* ¹⁷*And he was afraid, and said, "How awesome is this place! This is none other than the house of God, and this is the gate of heaven."*

¹⁸*So Jacob rose early in the morning, and he took the stone that he had put under his head and set it up for a pillar and poured oil on the top of it.* ¹⁹*He called that place Bethel; but the name of the city was Luz at the first.* ²⁰*Then Jacob made a vow, saying, "If God will be with me, and will keep me in this way that I go,*

and will give me bread to eat and clothing to wear ²¹*so that I come again to my father's house in peace, then the Lord shall be my God,* ²²*and this stone, which I have set up for a pillar, shall be God's house; and of all that you give me I will surely give one tenth to you."*

GENESIS 32:24–30 ²⁴*Jacob was left alone; and a man wrestled with him until daybreak.* ²⁵*When the man saw that he did not prevail against Jacob, he struck him on the hip socket; and Jacob's hip was put out of joint as he wrestled with him.* ²⁶*Then he said, "Let me go, for the day is breaking." But Jacob said, "I will not let you go, unless you bless me."* ²⁷*So he said to him, "What is your name?" And he said, "Jacob."* ²⁸*Then the man said, "You shall no longer be called Jacob, but Israel, for you have striven with God and with humans, and have prevailed."* ²⁹*Then Jacob asked him, "Please tell me your name." But he said, "Why is it that you ask my name?" And there he blessed him.* ³⁰*So Jacob called the place Peniel, saying, "For I have seen God face to face, and yet my life is preserved."*

These two angelic encounters of Jacob were separated by about two decades. The dream of the ladder with angels ascending and descending occurred in Jacob's young adulthood, after he had deceptively stolen the blessing and birthright of his dying father from his older brother, Esau. Jacob was fleeing from Esau's fury and had stopped for the night while making the long journey to the land of his exile in Haran. The second encounter, the night of divine wrestling, occurred after Jacob had married twice, produced twelve children, and was returning to his native land. Jacob's return to his ancestral homeland would involve meeting his brother Esau and taking up his responsibility as bearer of the covenant with God.

As Jacob fled from the house of his parents and began his life as a fugitive, he must have felt guilty, despairing, and abandoned. Through the revelation of the ladder (or stairway) traversed by God's angels, God gave comfort and hope to Jacob. When Jacob thought he traveled alone with survival as his only purpose, God assured him that the resources of heaven are available to those on earth. God offered this hopeless fugitive an alternative and optimistic future. He confirmed to Jacob the promises given to his father Isaac and his grandfather Abraham: land, countless offspring, and blessings to all the people of the earth (28:13–14). Then God gave three additional promises to address Jacob's present anxiety: God would be with him, protect him wherever he went, and bring him back to his own land. The ladder with God's angels traveling between heaven and earth was a powerful sign of these promises and of God's assurance to Jacob: "I will not leave you" (28:15).

Profoundly shaken by this awesome experience of divine presence, Jacob established the site as a shrine. He realized that in that place the gulf between heaven and earth had been joined by the angels. Declaring the place to be the "house of God" and the "gateway to heaven," Jacob set up the stone on which he had laid his head during his dream as a monument to the divine revelation and promises. He called the place Bethel (meaning "house of God"), and the Israelites came to worship God there in later centuries. Jacob realized there that he had a purpose and a destination, and the angelic vision of that night would sustain him through years of lonely exile.

Twenty years later, returning to his homeland with family and prosperity, Jacob faced an internal and external confrontation with his unresolved conflicts. He was filled with anxiety at the prospect of meeting his brother after so many years, fearing his anger and retaliation. But before Jacob could deal with his brother and carry on the tasks of mature adulthood, he had to deal with God. This divine encounter is described as a nocturnal struggle, a wrestling match in the darkness until dawn (32:24). It seems to be a nearly even match. Jacob is injured, but not defeated.

Who is the "man" with whom Jacob struggled? Is it his departed father Isaac, from whom he had wrested a blessing? Is it his twin brother Esau, with whom he wrestled even in his mother's womb? Is it his own shadow self, that darker part of his psyche filled with shame and fear which he must integrate before he could be whole? Or, as interpreted in later tradition (Hosea 12:4), is it an angel of God, enabling Jacob to recognize the transforming power of God and accept his spiritual destiny? The "man" with whom he wrestled is probably all of these. In the mysterious struggle Jacob is radically changed and matured. He had asked for a blessing; what he got was a new identity, expressed by a new name (32:26–28). He had been named Jacob ("trickster"); now he is Israel ("God struggles" or "he who struggles with God"). Because of his struggle, he is able to be reconciled with Esau and to fulfill his destiny as patriarch of a great people who will bring the blessings of God to the world.

Many centuries later, Jesus himself will describe the vision of faith in terms of the angels in Jacob's dream: "Very truly, I tell you, you will see heaven opened and the angels of God ascending and descending upon the Son of

Man" (John 1:51). Jesus himself is the mediator between heaven and earth. He is the "house of God," God's dwelling place on earth, and he is the "gateway to heaven." The revelation and promises given to Jacob achieve their highest fulfillment in Christ, the Word made flesh and dwelling among us.

Reflection and discussion

• When has God lowered a ladder into my life when I had nearly despaired of finding an exit?

• What does Jacob gain by wrestling with God that could not be obtained through a more tranquil encounter?

• When have I struggled with God, angels, and people (32:28)? Have I prevailed or been defeated? What have I gained in the struggle?

Prayer

God of Abraham, Isaac, and Jacob, you promise your blessings on life's journey and give me a purpose and a destination. Send me ladders to climb out of my despair and angels to show me the way to wholeness and maturity.

There the angel of the Lord appeared to him in a flame of fire out of a bush; he looked, and the bush was blazing, yet it was not consumed. Exod 3:2

Angel in the Blazing Fire

EXODUS 3:1–6 *¹Moses was keeping the flock of his father-in-law Jethro, the priest of Midian; he led his flock beyond the wilderness, and came to Horeb, the mountain of God. ²There the angel of the Lord appeared to him in a flame of fire out of a bush; he looked, and the bush was blazing, yet it was not consumed. ³Then Moses said, "I must turn aside and look at this great sight, and see why the bush is not burned up." ⁴When the Lord saw that he had turned aside to see, God called to him out of the bush, "Moses, Moses!" And he said, "Here I am." ⁵Then he said, "Come no closer! Remove the sandals from your feet, for the place on which you are standing is holy ground." ⁶He said further, "I am the God of your father, the God of Abraham, the God of Isaac, and the God of Jacob." And Moses hid his face, for he was afraid to look at God.*

EXODUS 23:20–25 *²⁰I am going to send an angel in front of you, to guard you on the way and to bring you to the place that I have prepared. ²¹Be attentive to him and listen to his voice; do not rebel against him, for he will not pardon your transgression; for my name is in him. ²²But if you listen attentively to his voice and do all that I say, then I will be an enemy to your enemies and a foe to your foes. ²³When my angel goes in front of you, and brings you to the Amorites, the Hittites, the Perizzites, the Canaanites, the Hivites, and the Jebusites, and I blot them out, ²⁴you shall not bow down to their gods, or worship them, or follow their practices, but you shall utterly demolish them and break their pillars in* *pieces.* ²⁵*You shall worship the Lord your God, and I will bless your bread and your water; and I will take sickness away from among you.*

G od called Moses through the mediation of "the angel of the Lord." The angel appeared to Moses in a flame of fire (3:2). The reader is told more than Moses knows at first. Moses sees a blazing bush that is not being burned up. Out of wonderment, Moses is drawn toward the bush to see why it is not consumed. After God opened the eyes of Moses to see, he then opened his ears to hear and called out his name. God then opened his mouth to speak: "Here I am" (3:4).

Fire was a primary medium for manifestations of God throughout the Bible. God appeared to Abraham as a flaming torch to establish the covenant (Gen 15:17). In the book of Exodus, God descended to Mount Sinai in fire (19:18), and Israel was guided through the wilderness at night by a pillar of fire (13:21). The book of Deuteronomy describes God's people gathered at God's mountain: "Then the Lord spoke to you out of the fire" (Deut 4:12). The book of Hebrews describes the blazing characteristics of God: "Indeed our God is a consuming fire" (Heb 12:29). Just as fire is ethereal and mysterious, so too is God spiritual and inscrutable. And just as fire is always flickering and changing its shape, so is God indefinable and always beyond our grasp.

Fire also frequently accompanies the descriptions of angels in the Bible. The book of Hebrews, in a quotation from Psalm 104:4, says that God's angels take the form of wind and fire: "He makes his angels winds, and his servants flames of fire" (Heb 1:7). God uses the elements of the material world for clothing that which is purely spiritual. Nature serves as God's instrument to communicate God's mystery, holiness, and passion. The fiery angel flaming from the bush joins the divine world to the material earth and allows Moses to hear the voice of God. In a flame of fire, God's messenger speaks to Moses a message that is both from God and from within the world. The voice is not disembodied; the messenger of the Lord indeed appeared and spoke. The rabbis describe this as divine condescension: God made his presence lowly in order to give room for his people to enter into a genuine conversation about the shape of the future.

Because God sent his angel to make his presence and voice known to Moses, the place becomes "holy ground" (3:5). This mountain, an ordinary part of the natural world, is sanctified because of the special purpose for which it is set apart by God. Here God would bring to a climax what he began with the call of Moses as he gives Moses the covenant code of Israel on the mountain. God said, "When you have brought the people out of Egypt, you shall worship God on this mountain" (3:12).

God also sent his angel as a guardian and guide for the people on their journey to the Promised Land (23:20; 32:34; 33:2). The presence of the angel was manifested by the pillar of cloud and fire which accompanied the people along the way. Because God said of the angel, "My name is in him" (23:21), the people are commanded to be attentive to the angel and to listen to his voice. The voice and presence of the angel is the mediated presence of God himself.

One of the primary functions of angels is to guide, protect, and accompany people traveling from one place to another. Like the Israelites who were attended by God's angel on their journey through the desert, we are directed and guarded by angels along the journey of life. Though the passage of our lives begins and ends in God, the earthly sojourn in between is sometimes like the wilderness. The words of God to Israel is a comforting message to us as well: "I am going to send an angel in front of you, to guard you on the way and to bring you to the place that I have prepared" (23:20).

Reflection and discussion

• Why is fire a primary symbol for manifesting God and his angels?

• What places are "holy ground" for me? What has made those places holy?

• In what other ways besides burning bushes does nature communicate God's mystery, holiness, and passion?

• What is another example of "divine condescension"?

• How has God guided and guarded me so far along the journey of life?

Prayer

God of Israel, you sent your angel to raise up the leadership of Moses and to guide your people through the wilderness into the Promised Land. May your angel guide, protect, and accompany me along my journey through this life and bring me safely home to the place you have prepared for me.

The commander of the army of the Lord said to Joshua, "Remove the sandals from your feet, for the place where you stand is holy." Josh 5:15

Horses and Chariots of Fire

JOSHUA 5:13–15 *¹³Once when Joshua was by Jericho, he looked up and saw a man standing before him with a drawn sword in his hand. Joshua went to him and said to him, "Are you one of us, or one of our adversaries?" ¹⁴He replied, "Neither; but as commander of the army of the Lord I have now come." And Joshua fell on his face to the earth and worshiped, and he said to him, "What do you command your servant, my lord?" ¹⁵The commander of the army of the Lord said to Joshua, "Remove the sandals from your feet, for the place where you stand is holy." And Joshua did so.*

2 KINGS 6:15–23 *¹⁵When an attendant of the man of God [Elisha] rose early in the morning and went out, an army with horses and chariots was all around the city. His servant said, "Alas, master! What shall we do?" ¹⁶He replied, "Do not be afraid, for there are more with us than there are with them." ¹⁷Then Elisha prayed: "O Lord, please open his eyes that he may see." So the Lord opened the eyes of the servant, and he saw; the mountain was full of horses and chariots of fire all around Elisha. ¹⁸When the Arameans came down against him, Elisha prayed to the Lord, and said, "Strike this people, please, with blindness." So he struck them with blindness as Elisha had asked. ¹⁹Elisha said to them, "This is not the way, and this is not the city; follow me, and I will bring you to the man whom you seek." And he led them to Samaria.*

²⁰As soon as they entered Samaria, Elisha said, "O Lord, open the eyes of these men so that they may see." The Lord opened their eyes, and they saw that they were inside Samaria. ²¹*When the king of Israel saw them he said to Elisha, "Father, shall I kill them? Shall I kill them?"* ²²*He answered, "No! Did you capture with your sword and your bow those whom you want to kill? Set food and water before them so that they may eat and drink; and let them go to their master."* ²³*So he prepared for them a great feast; after they ate and drank, he sent them on their way, and they went to their master. And the Arameans no longer came raiding into the land of Israel.*

Just as Moses received a revelation from God through an angel at the beginning of his career as leader of Israel (Exod 3), so too Joshua, as the successor to Moses, experienced an angelic revelation as he began a new period of Israel's history. The period of the Exodus was complete after God's angel guided the people to the Promised Land. Here the period of Conquest begins as Joshua leads the Israelites to acquire the land they had been promised (Josh 1:1–3).

Before the first battle, Joshua looked up and saw "a man standing before him with a drawn sword in his hand" (Josh 5:13). The man was neither an Israelite nor an adversary, but he identified himself as "commander of the army of the Lord." With that Joshua realized that the man was a heavenly presence and he bowed with his face to the ground in worship. The appearance is both a divine sanction for Joshua's new role as Israel's leader and the assurance of divine leadership for the military campaign upon which the Israelites are about to embark.

The account parallels the call of Moses, from Joshua's looking up at the angelic manifestation to the divine command to "remove the sandals from your feet, for the place where you stand is holy" (Josh 5:15). Joshua is indeed the divinely appointed successor to Moses. The commander of the Lord's army is probably the angel God sent to guide and protect Israel along the journey in the wilderness (Exod 23:20) who has now been sent for the next task in salvation-history. God's protective angel will guide the Israelites in the Promised Land just as he had guided them through the wilderness.

Several centuries later, during the period of Israel's monarchy, the nation was being attacked by Aramean troops. Hoping to capture God's prophet Elisha, a great army of troops came to the city of Dothan at night. With the light of dawn, Elisha's servant saw the horses and chariots of the enemy surrounding the city and grew fearful. But with calm confidence the prophet reassured his servant and said, "Do not be afraid, for there are more with us than there are with them" (2 Kings 6:16).

The source of Elisha's serenity became evident to the servant after Elisha prayed that God open his servant's eyes to see the fullness of reality. With eyes now able to see both the visible and the invisible, the servant saw the mountain ablaze with a divine army—"horses and chariots of fire all around" (2 Kings 6:17). With full vision, both Elisha and his servant know that the angels of God are present in overwhelming numbers as their defenders. The prophet then prays that God close the eyes of the enemy. Blinded, the troops are confused and brought to Samaria. When Elisha then prayed that God open the eyes of the enemy, the Arameans realized they were in Israel's capital city standing before the king. Though the king wanted to kill the enemy troops, Elisha demanded that he offer them a meal and then send them back to their home. Humbled and grateful, the Arameans no longer made war on the Israelites.

The fearful servant represents the reader in this episode. We have the possibility of seeing beyond the limitations of the present world to the fullness of reality. Through the theme of opened and closed eyes, blindness and vision, the narrative challenges us to realize that God's help is always available to us. The majesty of the angels is nothing less than the saving power of God, ever present though often invisible. When our present existence seems overwhelming, we can recall the words of Elisha: "There are more with us than there are with them."

Reflection and discussion

• What is the meaning of "neither" in Joshua 5:14? What is the difference between God being on our side and our being on God's side?

• When has my inability to see the full reality of a situation made me fearful and doubtful?

• What would I be able to see more clearly if I were blessed with the gift of deeper vision and greater insight?

• Why is Elisha's strategy of mercy more effective than violence (2 Kings 6:21–23)?

Prayer

> God of the heavenly hosts, you surround me with legions of angels ablaze with divine fire. Open my eyes to see the fullness of reality, the invisible world that is also the work of your saving love. When the forces of hostility and temptation seem to dominate, help me to realize that there are more with us than there are with them.

In the middle of the living creatures there was something that looked like burning coals of fire, like torches moving to and fro among the living creatures; the fire was bright, and lightning issued from the fire. Ezek 1:13

Seraphim and Cherubim

ISAIAH 6:1–8 *¹In the year that King Uzziah died, I saw the Lord sitting on a throne, high and lofty; and the hem of his robe filled the temple. ²Seraphs were in attendance above him; each had six wings: with two they covered their faces, and with two they covered their feet, and with two they flew. ³And one called to another and said:*

"Holy, holy, holy is the Lord of hosts;
the whole earth is full of his glory."

⁴The pivots on the thresholds shook at the voices of those who called, and the house filled with smoke. ⁵And I said: "Woe is me! I am lost, for I am a man of unclean lips, and I live among a people of unclean lips; yet my eyes have seen the King, the Lord of hosts!"

⁶Then one of the seraphs flew to me, holding a live coal that had been taken from the altar with a pair of tongs. ⁷The seraph touched my mouth with it and said: "Now that this has touched your lips, your guilt has departed and your sin is blotted out." ⁸Then I heard the voice of the Lord saying, "Whom shall I send, and who will go for us?" And I said, "Here am I; send me!"

EZEKIEL 1:4–14 *⁴As I looked, a stormy wind came out of the north: a great cloud with brightness around it and fire flashing forth continually, and in the middle of the fire, something like gleaming amber. ⁵In the middle of it was some-*

thing like four living creatures. This was their appearance: they were of human form. ⁶Each had four faces, and each of them had four wings. ⁷Their legs were straight, and the soles of their feet were like the sole of a calf's foot; and they sparkled like burnished bronze. ⁸Under their wings on their four sides they had human hands. And the four had their faces and their wings thus: ⁹their wings touched one another; each of them moved straight ahead, without turning as they moved. ¹⁰As for the appearance of their faces: the four had the face of a human being, the face of a lion on the right side, the face of an ox on the left side, and the face of an eagle; ¹¹such were their faces. Their wings were spread out above; each creature had two wings, each of which touched the wing of another, while two covered their bodies. ¹²Each moved straight ahead; wherever the spirit would go, they went, without turning as they went. ¹³In the middle of the living creatures there was something that looked like burning coals of fire, like torches moving to and fro among the living creatures; the fire was bright, and lightning issued from the fire. ¹⁴The living creatures darted to and fro, like a flash of lightning.

The seraphim (Hebrew plural of seraph) and cherubim (Hebrew plural of cherub) are angelic creatures who attend the throne of God and make up part of God's royal court. They are described in the Bible as magnificent and powerful creatures (a far cry from the baby cherubs of baroque art and valentine imagery). Seraphim literally means "fiery beings," creatures that shine brightly in God's presence and burn with God's brilliance. Cherubim means "intercessors" or "gatekeepers." Both seraphim and cherubim are described as winged creatures, the primary influence on the artistic convention giving wings to all angels. Though these beings are not called "angels" in the Bible, they are classified as angels in later Jewish and Christian tradition because they share in the function of angels as intermediaries between God and humanity.

Isaiah's vision in the temple of Jerusalem profoundly changes his inner and outer life. He sees God enthroned in royal garments amidst his heavenly court (Isa 6:1–2). The seraphim who attend God's throne have six wings each: two protect their faces from the brilliance of God's glory, two modestly cover their feet (a euphemism for sexual parts), and two for flying, propelling them to do whatever God calls them to do. The antiphonal chant of the seraphs (Isa 6:3) emphasizes God's holiness, the predominant divine quality throughout Isaiah's prophecies. The "glory" that fills "the whole earth" is God's visible splendor made known in creation. This Trishagion ("Thrice Holy") is the Hebrew superlative: God alone is most holy. The words of this heavenly liturgy, a chant still sung in Christian liturgical rites today, probably reflect an acclamation sung in Israel's temple period.

The holiness of God, which shook the temple and filled it with smoke, awed Isaiah and made him aware of his own unholiness. A seraph then flew to the prophet and touched his lips with a burning coal from the altar, effecting the cleansing of his sin (Isa 6:5–7). The seraphim perform both a prophetic function in proclaiming God's holiness and a priestly function in purifying Isaiah's guilt. The prophet is now able to hear God's call and respond with ready service: "Here I am; send me!" Isaiah teaches us that, despite an overwhelming sense of our own unworthiness, our understanding of God's direction for our lives will open up after an extended experience of worshiping the living God.

The transcendent vision of Ezekiel, marking his call to the prophetic office, is described amidst a thunderstorm with extensive lightning. Like the calls of Moses and Isaiah, it is marked by mysterious flames which express the awesome power of God breaking into the prophet's life and consciousness (Ezek 1:4, 13–14). In the midst of the flashing fire, he saw four creatures. Each was human in form but with four faces and four wings. Two of their wings were spread out, each touching the wings of another, and two of their wings covered their bodies. Their faces were like those of a human being in front, an eagle at the back, a lion and ox on either side (Ezek 1:4 11). They darted about like lightning flashing, constantly moving like flickering fire, and they supported the throne of God. Though they are called "living creatures" in this passage, later on in Ezekiel's descriptions, they are identified as "cherubim" (Ezek 10:15, 20).

Throughout the Old Testament, the God of Israel is described as the One "enthroned on/upon/above the cherubim" (1 Sam 4:4; 2 Sam 6:2; 2 Kings 19:15; 1 Chron 13:6; Ps 80:1; Ps 99:1; Isa 37:16). In the holy of holies of the wilderness tabernacle and in Solomon's temple, two gold-covered images of cherubim were placed on each side of the "mercy seat" above the ark of the covenant. Here God was present with his people, amidst the outstretched wings of the cherubim (Exod 25:17–22; 1 Kings 6:23–28). In the temple of Jerusalem God's people could imagine the gleaming golden cherubim, their outer wings touching each wall of the holy of holies and their inner wings touching one another, standing in silent witness to God's awesome majesty in the place on his earthly dwelling. Those Israelite voices raised a confident song in times of trouble: "The Lord is king; let the peoples tremble! He sits enthroned upon the cherubim; let the earth quake!" (Ps 99:1). The cherubim of gold reminded them that God on his throne is surrounded by glorious, worshiping angels, their faces turned toward him, ready to do his will.

Reflection and discussion

• What angelic qualities are shared by the cherubim and seraphim?

• How might Isaiah's experience of God in the temple have changed his inner and outer life?

Prayer

Holy, holy, holy is the Lord of hosts. Heaven and earth are full of your glory. God, enthroned upon the cherubim, cleanse me from the guilt of sin and send me with confidence to do your will.

Suddenly there was a great earthquake; for an angel of the Lord, descending from heaven, came and rolled back the stone and sat on it. His appearance was like lightning, and his clothing white as snow. Matt 28:2–3

Heralds of the Mystery of Christ

LUKE 2:8–15 *8In that region there were shepherds living in the fields, keeping watch over their flock by night. 9Then an angel of the Lord stood before them, and the glory of the Lord shone around them, and they were terrified. 10But the angel said to them, "Do not be afraid; for see—I am bringing you good news of great joy for all the people: 11to you is born this day in the city of David a Savior, who is the Messiah, the Lord. 12This will be a sign for you: you will find a child wrapped in bands of cloth and lying in a manger." 13And suddenly there was with the angel a multitude of the heavenly host, praising God and saying,*

14"Glory to God in the highest heaven,
and on Earth peace among those whom he favors!"

15When the angels had left them and gone into heaven, the shepherds said to one another, "Let us go now to Bethlehem and see this thing that has taken place, which the Lord has made known to us."

MATTHEW 28:1–8 *1After the sabbath, as the first day of the week was dawning, Mary Magdalene and the other Mary went to see the tomb. 2And suddenly there was a great earthquake; for an angel of the Lord, descending from heaven, came and rolled back the stone and sat on it. 3His appearance was like lightning,* *and his clothing white as snow.* ⁴*For fear of him the guards shook and became like dead men.* ⁵*But the angel said to the women, "Do not be afraid; I know that you are looking for Jesus who was crucified.* ⁶*He is not here; for he has been raised, as he said. Come, see the place where he lay.* ⁷*Then go quickly and tell his disciples, 'He has been raised from the dead, and indeed he is going ahead of you to Galilee; there you will see him.' This is my message for you."* ⁸*So they left the tomb quickly with fear and great joy, and ran to tell his disciples.*

The work of the angels as heavenly messengers is highlighted in the Bible at strategic times and places in the history of redemption. But none is so important as the role of the angels as messengers of God at the birth and resurrection of Jesus. At these two climactic moments of humanity's salvation, angels appear to interpret the meaning of the events for those present at the moment and for all who read the gospel narratives through the ages.

The appearance of an angel in the biblical narratives is not a heart-warming experience, filled with charming sweetness. It is a petrifying event. When an angel appeared at night to the shepherds watching their flock in the fields around Bethlehem, Luke's narrative says, "they were terrified" (Luke 2:9). When the angel came to the empty tomb in Jerusalem at early dawn, the soldiers guarding the tomb experienced a paralyzing fear: "For fear of him the guards shook and became like dead men" (Matt 28:4). Yet, both to the shepherds and to the women who came to the tomb, the angel offered the comforting reassurance given to people throughout the Bible who experience a divine encounter: "Do not be afraid" (Luke 2:10; Matt 28:5). In each scene, the angel then interprets the meaning of the event, offers them a sign, and then sends them on a mission.

In Luke's account of the birth of Jesus, the angel of God proclaims "good news of great joy for all the people." In explaining that the child born in David's city is Savior, Messiah, and Lord, the angel sums up the whole message of the gospel (Luke 2:11). As Savior, Jesus will rescue humanity from sin and heal the divisions that separate people from God and one another. As Messiah, Jesus is the anointed heir of David, the one who will establish God's kingdom. As Lord, Jesus is proclaimed with the same divine title as God himself. The sign confirming the angel's announcement is "a child wrapped in bands of cloth and lying in a manger." The simplicity of the sign is a strong contrast with the regal identity of the child that the angel just proclaimed. The angel invites the shepherds and all the readers of the gospel to contemplate the humility and the majesty of this newborn child.

The angel is joined by a throng of the heavenly chorus praising God at the announcement of Christ's birth. The canticle of the angels, the Gloria (Luke 2:14), may have been a refrain sung by the early Christians in their worship. It proclaims that heaven has touched earth in this wondrous birth. God in heaven is given glory; people on earth are brought peace. This good news of joy and peace announced by the angels anticipates the good news that will unfold throughout the narrative of Jesus' life, death, and resurrection. The angels prefigure the church following the resurrection, a community of disciples who will proclaim the gospel to the world.

In Matthew's account of the resurrection of Jesus, the bright and dazzling angel descended from heaven, rolled back the stone, and sat upon it (Matt 28:2–3). These actions of the heavenly messenger indicate that the resurrection is a divine achievement, God's triumph over death. The angel announces the good news for those seeking the body of their crucified master: "He is not here; for he has been raised, as he said" (Matt 28:6). The sign confirming the angel's announcement is "the place where he lay." In contrast to the sign that accompanied Christ's birth, the child wrapped in bands of cloth and lying in a manger, the bands of cloth that wrapped Christ in death no longer bound his Risen body and he no longer lay in the place where his body was placed.

The angel sends the women on the church's first evangelizing mission, to proclaim the good news of Christ's resurrection. The command to "go quickly" expresses the urgency of the news. The "fear and great joy" of the women expresses the mixed emotions of their heart as they "ran to tell the disciples" (Matt 28:7–8). As the first messengers of the gospel, the two women anticipate the evangelizing message destined to be preached to all people.

Reflection and discussion

• What are the most important meanings of Christ's birth and resurrection for me?

• In what ways do my Christmas and Easter decorations include angels?

• Of all the people the angels could have visited, why did God send them to the shepherds and to the women?

• In what way do the women at the tomb anticipate the church's mission of evangelization?

Prayer

Jesus, born into our world and risen from the dead, you have enriched human life in your coming among us and conquered our worst enemy and deepest fear in being raised to life. Help me to appreciate the wondrous gifts of your Incarnation and your Resurrection.

Of the angels he says, "He makes his angels winds, and his servants flames of fire." Heb 1:7

Spirits in Divine Service

HEBREWS 1:1–14 ¹*Long ago God spoke to our ancestors in many and various ways by the prophets, ²but in these last days he has spoken to us by a Son, whom he appointed heir of all things, through whom he also created the worlds. ³He is the reflection of God's glory and the exact imprint of God's very being, and he sustains all things by his powerful word. When he had made purification for sins, he sat down at the right hand of the Majesty on high, ⁴having become as much superior to angels as the name he has inherited is more excellent than theirs.*

⁵*For to which of the angels did God ever say,*

"You are my Son;

today I have begotten you"?

Or again,

"I will be his Father,

and he will be my Son"?

⁶*And again, when he brings the firstborn into the world, he says,*

"Let all God's angels worship him."

⁷*Of the angels he says,*

"He makes his angels winds,

and his servants flames of fire."

⁸*But of the Son he says,*

"Your throne, O God, is forever and ever,

and the righteous scepter is the scepter of your kingdom.
⁹*You have loved righteousness and hated wickedness;*
therefore God, your God, has anointed you
  with the oil of gladness beyond your companions."
¹⁰*And,*
  "In the beginning, Lord, you founded the earth,
    and the heavens are the work of your hands;
  ¹¹*they will perish, but you remain;*
    they will all wear out like clothing;
  ¹²*like a cloak you will roll them up,*
    and like clothing they will be changed.
    But you are the same,
      and your years will never end."
¹³*But to which of the angels has he ever said,*
  "Sit at my right hand
    until I make your enemies a footstool for your feet"?
¹⁴*Are not all angels spirits in the divine service, sent to serve for the sake of those*
who are to inherit salvation?

At the time the New Testament was written, there was great interest in angels in Jewish religious thinking. Some Jews, knowing that angels are mediators between God and humanity, thought that Jesus himself was an angel. Others understood angels to be divine beings to be worshiped. The author of Hebrews wanted to clarify the role of God's angels in relationship to Christ. As wonderful as the angels are, their role in God's plan is completely different and subordinate to that of Christ. The angels are created beings whose purpose is to worship God and his Son and to serve those who will inherit salvation.

Much of Hebrews elucidates the distinction between the ways that God spoke to former generations, and the definitive, climactic, and decisive word God has spoken through Jesus, his Son (verses 1–2). All that God revealed in earlier times was preparatory for Christ, the goal and ultimate meaning of all that came before him. As "the reflection of God's glory" and as "the exact imprint of God's very being" (verse 3), the Son is not a part of God's creation but is the manifestation of God's very essence. He is the one through whom God made all that exists and the one who sustains the universe and keeps it going. As the one who "sat down at the right hand of the Majesty on high" (verse 4), the Son of God shares in God's rule with all creation, even the angels, in submission to him.

The remaining verses of this first chapter of Hebrews consists of a constellation of seven quotations from the Old Testament, all in service of elaborating the point that Jesus, the Son, is "much superior to angels" (verse 4). The Scriptures in which God addresses "my Son" are spoken about Christ alone (verse 5); God never spoke so gloriously of angels. The angels, rather, are called to bow down before the Son (verse 6).

Quoting from the Greek version of Psalm 104, the author implies that God's angels are manifested through the natural elements of wind and fire: "He makes his angels winds, and his servants flames of fire" (verse 7). Yet when compared to verses about the permanent power and everlasting majesty of the Son (verses 8–12), the angels seem to be fleeting and transitory. Like the wind, they exert their force but then pass away; like flames, they burn with power but then flicker out.

The angels are certainly God's spiritual agents, but they are distinctly subordinate servants, not to be likened to God or his Son (verse 14). As awesome and powerful as the angels are in doing God's will and in bringing about the salvation God offers, we must keep them in perspective. God and his Son are the source of our salvation. By God's grace, the angels serve us toward that end.

Reflection and discussion

• Why is it important to have a clear understanding of the nature and purpose of angels in God's plan?

• Why would some have thought Jesus to be an angel?

• What are some of the ways in which the Son is superior to the angels?

• What have I learned about angels so far that is particularly encouraging to me?

Prayer

Heavenly Son of God, your desire is to save us from death and lead us to eternal life with you. Send your ministering angels to my aid and give me the grace I need to respond to your plan for my life.

SUGGESTIONS FOR FACILITATORS, GROUP SESSION 2

1. If there are newcomers who were not present for the first group session, introduce them now.

2. You may want to pray this prayer as a group:

Lord God, throughout the long history of our salvation, you have sent your angels as mediators of your presence. From the stories of Jacob, to the calling of Moses, through the history of Israel, to the coming of your Son, your angels have connected heaven and earth and manifested your presence. With the perfect mediation of your Son, your angels announce his salvation and lead us to share more fully in his life. As we gather as your people, encourage us to listen to your word, allow it to penetrate our hearts, and give us the confidence necessary to put it into practice in our daily lives.

3. Ask one or more of the following questions:
   - What was your biggest challenge in Bible study over this past week?
   - What did you learn about God's angels from your study this week?
   - What did you learn about yourself this week?

4. Discuss lessons 1 through 6 together. Assuming that group members have read the Scripture and commentary during the week, there is no need to read it aloud. As you review each lesson, you might want to briefly summarize the Scripture passages of each lesson and ask the group what stands out most clearly from the commentary.

5. Choose one or more of the questions for reflection and discussion from each lesson to talk over as a group. You may want to ask group members which question was most challenging or helpful to them as you review each lesson.

6. Keep the discussion moving, but don't rush the discussion in order to complete more questions. Allow time for the questions that provoke the most discussion.

7. Instruct group members to complete lessons 7 through 12 on their own during the six days before the next group meeting. They should write out their own answers to the questions as preparation for next week's group discussion.

8. Conclude by praying aloud together the prayer at the end of lesson 6, or any other prayer you choose.

Do not neglect to show hospitality to strangers, for by doing that some have entertained angels without knowing it. Heb 13:2

Messengers to Abraham and Sarah

GENESIS 18:1–16 *¹The Lord appeared to Abraham by the oaks of Mamre, as he sat at the entrance of his tent in the heat of the day. ²He looked up and saw three men standing near him. When he saw them, he ran from the tent entrance to meet them, and bowed down to the ground. ³He said, "My lord, if I find favor with you, do not pass by your servant. ⁴Let a little water be brought, and wash your feet, and rest yourselves under the tree. ⁵Let me bring a little bread, that you may refresh yourselves, and after that you may pass on—since you have come to your servant." So they said, "Do as you have said." ⁶And Abraham hastened into the tent to Sarah, and said, "Make ready quickly three measures of choice flour, knead it, and make cakes." ⁷Abraham ran to the herd, and took a calf, tender and good, and gave it to the servant, who hastened to prepare it. ⁸Then he took curds and milk and the calf that he had prepared, and set it before them; and he stood by them under the tree while they ate.*

⁹They said to him, "Where is your wife Sarah?" And he said, "There, in the tent." ¹⁰Then one said, "I will surely return to you in due season, and your wife Sarah shall have a son." And Sarah was listening at the tent entrance behind him. ¹¹Now Abraham and Sarah were old, advanced in age; it had ceased to be with Sarah after the manner of women. ¹²So Sarah laughed to herself, saying, "After I have grown old, and my husband is old, shall I have pleasure?" ¹³The Lord said to

Abraham, "Why did Sarah laugh, and say, 'Shall I indeed bear a child, now that I am old?' ¹⁴*Is anything too wonderful for the Lord? At the set time I will return to you, in due season, and Sarah shall have a son."* ¹⁵*But Sarah denied, saying, "I did not laugh"; for she was afraid. He said, "Oh yes, you did laugh."*

¹⁶*Then the men set out from there, and they looked toward Sodom; and Abraham went with them to set them on their way.*

A t the beginning of this scene, the reader is informed that Abraham's visit by the three strangers is a divine revelation: "The Lord appeared to Abraham" (verse 1). However, nothing in the text suggests that Abraham recognizes his visitors as the angels they are later revealed to be (see 19:1). When Abraham looked up while sitting at the entrance of his tent he saw "three men" (verse 2). His extravagant hospitality was simply his characteristic response to strangers at his home. Offering them a place of rest and refreshment from the noonday heat, he prepared a feast for them. Bread made of finest flour, curds and milk, and a choice, tender calf made a first-rate spread to place before his guests. Because Abraham did not realize he was being visited by divine messengers, he did not take off his sandals, worship God, or build a shrine. Rather, Abraham's hospitality to strangers was itself an act of worship. As the Talmud states, "Hospitality to wayfarers is greater than welcoming the Divine Presence." And as the New Testament book of Hebrews advises, "Do not neglect to show hospitality to strangers, for by doing that some have entertained angels without knowing it" (Heb 13:2).

In the Bible angels frequently assume human form so that those to whom they appear are at first unaware of their angelic nature. The identity of Abraham's visitors is deliberately obscure in the narrative. In the opening scene (verses 2–8) as well as the departure (verse 16), it is "three men." But in verse 1 as well as the revelatory scene (verses 9–15), it is "the Lord." The three visitors and God himself speak interchangeably—sometimes the men speak and at other times the speaker is the Lord—indicating both God's nearness and his mysterious elusiveness.

The divine message delivered by the three angels is a birth announcement. Sarah, barren and past the age of childbearing by many decades, would have a son within the year (verses 10–11). Their closed world of barrenness is shattered by a new possibility that lies outside their rational prospects. Sarah's incredulous laughter expresses the tension between the inscrutable promise of God and human resistance (verses 12–13). The story shows us how diffi-cult faith is. It is not a reasonable act that fits into our normal expectations.

The key question of the passage is about the astonishing ways of God: "Is anything too wonderful for the Lord?" (verse 14). The question really is an invitation to faith, an open question that awaits an answer. If we respond, "Yes, some things are too wonderful for God," then we choose to live in a closed world where life is reliable and staid, and where hopelessness is nor-mal. If, on the other hand, we respond, "No, nothing is impossible with God," we place our trust radically in God and open ourselves to a life where any-thing is possible. With this kind of faith, we live life in receptive hopefulness, and any stranger can be a messenger from God.

Reflection and discussion

• Why do God and his angels speak interchangeably to Abraham and Sarah? What does this tell me about the function of angels?

• How do I answer the question, "Is anything too wonderful for the Lord?" (verse 14)?

Prayer

God of Abraham and Sarah, deepen my trust in you and open my life to new possibilities. Help me to experience your presence in the people I meet, especially in the wayfarer and the stranger, and to be ready to hear your message from them.

Then the angel of the Lord reached out the tip of the staff that was in his hand, and fire sprang up from the rock and consumed the meat and the unleavened cakes; and the angel of the Lord vanished from his sight.

Judg 6:21

Gideon Commissioned to Lead Israel

JUDGES 6:11–24 *[11]Now the angel of the Lord came and sat under the oak at Ophrah, which belonged to Joash the Abiezrite, as his son Gideon was beating out wheat in the wine press, to hide it from the Midianites. [12]The angel of the Lord appeared to him and said to him, "The Lord is with you, you mighty warrior." [13]Gideon answered him, "But sir, if the Lord is with us, why then has all this happened to us? And where are all his wonderful deeds that our ancestors recounted to us, saying, 'Did not the Lord bring us up from Egypt?' But now the Lord has cast us off, and given us into the hand of Midian." [14]Then the Lord turned to him and said, "Go in this might of yours and deliver Israel from the hand of Midian; I hereby commission you." [15]He responded, "But sir, how can I deliver Israel? My clan is the weakest in Manasseh, and I am the least in my family." [16]The Lord said to him, "But I will be with you, and you shall strike down the Midianites, every one of them." [17]Then he said to him, "If now I have found favor with you, then show me a sign that it is you who speak with me. [18]Do not depart from here until I come to you, and bring out my present, and set it before you." And he said, "I will stay until you return."*

[19]So Gideon went into his house and prepared a kid, and unleavened cakes

from an ephah of flour; the meat he put in a basket, and the broth he put in a pot, and brought them to him under the oak and presented them. [20] *The angel of God said to him, "Take the meat and the unleavened cakes, and put them on this rock, and pour out the broth." And he did so.* [21] *Then the angel of the Lord reached out the tip of the staff that was in his hand, and touched the meat and the unleavened cakes; and fire sprang up from the rock and consumed the meat and the unleavened cakes; and the angel of the Lord vanished from his sight.* [22] *Then Gideon perceived that it was the angel of the Lord; and Gideon said, "Help me, Lord God! For I have seen the angel of the Lord face to face."* [23] *But the Lord said to him, "Peace be to you; do not fear, you shall not die."* [24] *Then Gideon built an altar there to the Lord, and called it, The Lord is peace. To this day it still stands at Ophrah, which belongs to the Abiezrites.*

Following the conquest of the land and before the establishment of the monarchy, the Israelite tribes lived in the period of the judges. The tribes had not yet made their control over the land secure, and other peoples were making their own claims on the land and its produce. In the setting of this narrative, the Israelites had taken to the hills and were hiding in caves to escape the ravaging armies of Midian. Yet, when they cried out to God for help, God searched for a leader from among the Israelites to deliver his people from the Midianites.

When "the angel of the Lord" came to Gideon, he was threshing wheat in the wine press to hide the grain from the Midianites (verse 11). The call of Gideon bears many similarities to other calls, like those of Moses and Isaiah. The angel is God's messenger, but he also communicated the presence of God to Gideon. The angel's opening words, "The Lord is with you" (verse 12), assures Gideon of God's continuing presence with him but also informs him that God is with him now through the divine messenger. As in other accounts, the angel and God speak interchangeably; the words of the angel (verses 12, 29) and the words of the Lord (verses 14, 16, 23) are purposely alternated in order to indicate that the angel is God's representative, speaking only in behalf of God. By listening to the messenger, Gideon is listening to God.

The angel's assurance that God is present is met with Gideon's sharp reply. If God is with Israel, as in the noble past, there is certainly no evidence of that divine presence (verse 13). Gideon's commission as deliverer of Israel is given by the Lord: "Go in this might of yours and deliver Israel from the hand of

Midian; I hereby commission you" (verse 14). Like Moses and Isaiah, Gideon expressed his objections to the call, reservations stemming from his human feelings of inadequacy. But God assures him, "I will be with you" (verses 15–16). Gideon's strength is not his own; he will fight with the might of God. The book of Judges indicates throughout that Israel's future is not dependent on the nations potential or achievements, but is solely in the hands of God.

The call of Gideon concludes with his request for a conclusive sign of the divine authority with which he is to take up his mission. The sign becomes a sacrifice to God as the angel touches Gideon's offerings with the tip of his staff causing fire to spring up from the rock to consume the offerings (verses 17–21). Now Gideon knew for sure that he had encountered an angel of the Lord. The angel indeed represented God himself, yet at the same time, the angel was God's servant, always giving God praise. Gideon and the angel together offered the sacrifice to God, and then the angel vanished from Gideon's sight, indicating by his return to God that the sacrifice has been accepted by the Lord.

Gideon built an altar at the rock under the oak of Ophrah, the place where he had encountered God through his angel. Sanctified by the sacrifice of Gideon and the angel, the place was called Yahweh-Shalom (The Lord is Peace, verse 24) and became a place of worship. The sacrificial worship of Israel was a foretaste of the Eucharistic sacrifice of Christians. In Eucharist we enter into the realm of angelic mediation and ministry. Angels come into the visible world in order to take our offerings into the invisible; they transform earthly offerings into heavenly gifts. In one of the earliest Eucharistic prayers, the church prays "that your angel may take this sacrifice to your altar in heaven."

Reflection and discussion

• What are the similarities between the calls of Moses, Isaiah, and Gideon?

• Why was Gideon unsure whether he had been met by God's angel? When did Gideon realize that he had seen the angel of the Lord?

• Does God offer signs of his presence to me? How would I recognize a sign?

• What is the role of angels in the worship of God? How can recognizing the role of angels help me worship God better?

Prayer

God of ancient Israel, you have guided and protected your people from age to age. Save me from all who threaten me with harm. May the offering of my life, joined with the sacrificial death of your Son, be an acceptable sacrifice on your heavenly altar.

When the flame went up toward heaven from the altar, the angel of the Lord ascended in the flame of the altar while Manoah and his wife looked on; and they fell on their faces to the ground. Judg 13:20

Announcing the Birth of Samson

JUDGES 13:2–24 *²There was a certain man of Zorah, of the tribe of the Danites, whose name was Manoah. His wife was barren, having borne no children. ³And the angel of the Lord appeared to the woman and said to her, "Although you are barren, having borne no children, you shall conceive and bear a son. ⁴Now be careful not to drink wine or strong drink, or to eat anything unclean, ⁵for you shall conceive and bear a son. No razor is to come on his head, for the boy shall be a nazirite to God from birth. It is he who shall begin to deliver Israel from the hand of the Philistines." ⁶Then the woman came and told her husband, "A man of God came to me, and his appearance was like that of an angel of God, most awe-inspiring; I did not ask him where he came from, and he did not tell me his name; ⁷but he said to me, 'You shall conceive and bear a son. So then drink no wine or strong drink, and eat nothing unclean, for the boy shall be a nazirite to God from birth to the day of his death.'"*

⁸Then Manoah entreated the Lord, and said, "O, Lord, I pray, let the man of God whom you sent come to us again and teach us what we are to do concerning the boy who will be born." ⁹God listened to Manoah, and the angel of God came again to the woman as she sat in the field; but her husband Manoah was not with her. ¹⁰So the woman ran quickly and told her husband, "The man who came to me the other day has appeared to me." [11] *Manoah got up and followed his wife, and came to the man and said to him, "Are you the man who spoke to this woman?" And he said, "I am."* [12] *Then Manoah said, "Now when your words come true, what is to be the boy's rule of life; what is he to do?"* [13] *The angel of the Lord said to Manoah, "Let the woman give heed to all that I said to her.* [14] *She may not eat of anything that comes from the vine. She is not to drink wine or strong drink, or eat any unclean thing. She is to observe everything that I commanded her."*

[15] *Manoah said to the angel of the Lord, "Allow us to detain you, and prepare a kid for you."* [16] *The angel of the Lord said to Manoah, "If you detain me, I will not eat your food; but if you want to prepare a burnt offering, then offer it to the Lord." (For Manoah did not know that he was the angel of the Lord.)* [17] *Then Manoah said to the angel of the Lord, "What is your name, so that we may honor you when your words come true?"* [18] *But the angel of the Lord said to him, "Why do you ask my name? It is too wonderful."*

[19] *So Manoah took the kid with the grain offering, and offered it on the rock to the Lord, to him who works wonders.* [20] *When the flame went up toward heaven from the altar, the angel of the Lord ascended in the flame of the altar while Manoah and his wife looked on; and they fell on their faces to the ground.* [21] *The angel of the Lord did not appear again to Manoah and his wife. Then Manoah realized that it was the angel of the Lord.* [22] *And Manoah said to his wife, "We shall surely die, for we have seen God."* [23] *But his wife said to him, "If the Lord had meant to kill us, he would not have accepted a burnt offering and a grain offering at our hands, or shown us all these things, or now announced to us such things as these."*

[24] *The woman bore a son, and named him Samson. The boy grew, and the Lord blessed him.*

During the period of the judges, between the time of Moses and David, the Israelites were continually falling away from God and being assailed by their enemies. In this period God sent his angels as signs of his presence, to announce divine help for his people, and to assure them that he would never forsake his covenant.

The angel of the Lord appeared to the unnamed mother of Samson, the wife of Manoah. Like Sarah, the mother of Isaac and wife of Abraham, she "was barren, having borne no children" (verse 2). But the angel announced to her, "You shall conceive and bear a son" (verse 3). Samson, her son, was to be consecrated to God from the womb as a "nazirite," a vow associated with ritual purity required of those who fight God's battles. Since Samson was a nazirite from birth, his future struggles with the mighty Philistines would be the Lord's struggle.

When the woman told her husband about the encounter, she said, "A man of God came to me, and his appearance was like that of an angel of God, most awe-inspiring; I did not ask him where he came from, and he did not tell me his name" (verse 6). The Hebrew word translated here as "awe-inspiring" is often used to describe the terrifying and glorious majesty of God himself. Yet neither the woman nor her husband realized at first that the visitation was from God's angel. They were mystified that the "man of God" did not tell where he came from and refused to give his name.

Like Abraham with his three angelic messengers, Manoah offers hospitality to the visitor. The angel's reply hints that Manoah is entertaining an angel without knowing it (verses 15–16; see Heb 13:2). Manoah's question to the angel, "What is your name?" and the angel's reply, "Why do you ask my name?" is the same dialogue as between Jacob and the mysterious visitor with whom he wrestled in the night (Gen 32:29). Rather than be told the stranger's name, both Jacob and Manoah receive a blessing.

Manoah is told to prepare a holocaust, a sacrifice in which the offerings are burnt completely, and to offer it to the Lord. When he offers the sacrifice, Manoah and his wife witness a wondrous confirmation of the angel's message: "When the flame went up toward heaven from the altar, the angel of the Lord ascended in the flame of the altar while Manoah and his wife looked on; and they fell on their faces to the ground" (verse 20). In the ascent in the holy flame, God manifested his presence in his angel. Knowing they had seen God, Manoah feared for their lives. But his trusting wife knew that the angel's ascent in the flame was God's confirming sign of his presence and message through his angel (verses 22–23).

Reflection and discussion

• How does Manoah's wife describe to her husband the "man of God" who came to her? Why didn't she know he was God's angel?

• Compare and contrast the reactions of Manoah and his wife to the encounter with God's angel. Who seems to have the better insight?

• How can I better open my life to the ministry of angels?

Prayer

> Lord God, accept the sacrifice of my life, together with the offerings of your church throughout the world, to the praise and glory of your name. May your angel take this sacrifice, together with the eternal sacrifice of your Son, to your altar in heaven.

"I am Gabriel. I stand in the presence of God, and I have been sent to speak to you and to bring you this good news." Luke 1:19

Gabriel Sent to Herald Zechariah's Son

LUKE 1:5–20 *⁵In the days of King Herod of Judea, there was a priest named Zechariah, who belonged to the priestly order of Abijah. His wife was a descendant of Aaron, and her name was Elizabeth. ⁶Both of them were righteous before God, living blamelessly according to all the commandments and regulations of the Lord. ⁷But they had no children, because Elizabeth was barren, and both were getting on in years.*

⁸Once when he was serving as priest before God and his section was on duty, ⁹he was chosen by lot, according to the custom of the priesthood, to enter the sanctuary of the Lord and offer incense. ¹⁰Now at the time of the incense offering, the whole assembly of the people was praying outside. ¹¹Then there appeared to him an angel of the Lord, standing at the right side of the altar of incense. ¹²When Zechariah saw him, he was terrified; and fear overwhelmed him. ¹³But the angel said to him, "Do not be afraid, Zechariah, for your prayer has been heard. Your wife Elizabeth will bear you a son, and you will name him John. ¹⁴You will have joy and gladness, and many will rejoice at his birth, ¹⁵for he will be great in the sight of the Lord. He must never drink wine or strong drink; even before his birth he will be filled with the Holy Spirit. ¹⁶He will turn many of the people of Israel to the Lord their God. ¹⁷With the spirit and power of Elijah he will go before him, to turn the hearts of parents to their children, and the disobedient to the wisdom

of the righteous, to make ready a people prepared for the Lord." [18]*Zechariah said
to the angel, "How will I know that this is so? For I am an old man, and my wife
is getting on in years."* [19]*The angel replied, "I am Gabriel. I stand in the presence
of God, and I have been sent to speak to you and to bring you this good news.*
[20]*But now, because you did not believe my words, which will be fulfilled in their
time, you will become mute, unable to speak, until the day these things occur."*

The new era of salvation proclaimed in the gospel of Luke begins with
the angel's announcement to Zechariah of John the Baptist's conception. Like Abraham and Sarah at the dawn of salvation history,
Zechariah and his wife Elizabeth were elderly and without hope of having
children (verse 7). Yet throughout the Scriptures we see that God uses such
hopeless human conditions as the ground of new divine possibilities.
Zechariah and Elizabeth personified Jewish devotion at its best. There were
both from priestly families and each blamelessly following the law of God
(verses 5–6). Their faithful adherence to Israel's ancient institutions, rituals,
and beliefs put them in a position to be used for God's new purposes.

The annunciation to Zechariah follows the pattern of numerous birth
announcements from the Old Testament. First, the angel (or God) appears;
second, the recipient is troubled and fearful; third, reassurance is given and
the birth is announced; fourth, the recipient raises an objection; and fifth, a
confirming sign is given. This continuity with patterns familiar from the Old
Testament indicates that this is not just the account of one angelic appearance
to an old man, but a deeply significant part of God's whole plan of salvation.
God is working within the ancient faith of Israel to bring about the fulfillment of long-held expectations. The new era of salvation is heir to all that
God has already done through the covenanted life of Israel.

The angel of God appeared to Zechariah while he was serving as priest in
the temple at Jerusalem. No place was more representative of the presence
and promises of God. As the priest chosen by lot to make the incense offering, Zechariah entered the sanctuary and scattered incense on the burning
coals of the altar, a ritual prescribed in Exodus 30:7–8. The people attending
the offering stood outside the sanctuary in prayer, awaiting the priest's reap-
pearance and his blessing (verses 8–10).

When Zechariah saw the angel in the sanctuary, "standing at the right side
of the altar of incense," he was overwhelmed with terror (verses 11–12). But

the angel reassured him, telling him not to fear, "for your prayer has been heard." Since the answer to Zechariah's prayer is that his wife Elizabeth would bear a son, we may assume that Zechariah was praying for the gift of a child. But the words of the angel also refer to Zechariah's priestly prayer, the supplication of the people of Israel that God bring about the fulfillment of their longing. The assurance of the angel is that God does not forget his covenant.

Gabriel is one of the few angels mentioned by name in the Bible. The others are Michael and Raphael. These three, along with Uriel and three others whose names vary, are "the seven angels of the presence" spoken of in the Jewish literature of the time. The mention of Gabriel reminds the reader of the same angel's appearance in the book of Daniel. Gabriel came to Daniel "in swift flight," at the time of sacrifice in the temple (Dan 9:21). His appearance again here evokes the expectation that the times foretold by the prophets have arrived.

The angel's message to Zechariah is fourfold: Elizabeth will have a son to be named John (verse 13); he will bring joy and gladness to many (verse 14); he will be dedicated to God in the nazirite tradition, as was Samson (verse 15; Judg 13:2–5); and he will minister in the spirit and power of the prophet Elijah, who was expected to return and prepare God's people for the final days (verses 16–17; Mal 4:5–6).

Understandably, Zechariah has doubts, and because of his lack of belief he is struck speechless (verse 20). His silence leaves us with a mood of mysterious expectation, waiting for God's next move as the new age of salvation dawns. This pregnant elderly woman and this mute elderly man demonstrate that God reverses human expectations; the humanly impossible become possible with God. Her barren womb will give birth to the prophet of Israel's Messiah; his mute tongue will issue forth in praise to God.

Reflection and discussion

• What are some similarities between the angel's announcement to Zechariah and other angelic appearances in the Old Testament?

• What is Luke expressing by narrating this angelic annunciation with the same pattern as birth announcements of the Old Testament?

• Why did God punish Zechariah's doubt, while dealing patiently with the others' doubts?

• What did God do with Elizabeth's barrenness and Zechariah's disbelief? What can God do with my spiritual barrenness and disbelief?

Prayer

> *Lord our God, in every age you shatter limits and open lives to the vastness of your promises. Heal my spiritual barrenness and restore my faith in you so that my lips will proclaim your works and my life will witness your faithfulness.*

The angel said to her, "Do not be afraid, Mary, for you have found favor with God. And now, you will conceive in your womb and bear a son, and you will name him Jesus." Luke 1:30–31

Gabriel Sent By God to Mary

LUKE 1:26–38 *26In the sixth month the angel Gabriel was sent by God to a town in Galilee called Nazareth, 27to a virgin engaged to a man whose name was Joseph, of the house of David. The virgin's name was Mary. 28And he came to her and said, "Greetings, favored one! The Lord is with you." 29But she was much perplexed by his words and pondered what sort of greeting this might be. 30The angel said to her, "Do not be afraid, Mary, for you have found favor with God. 31And now, you will conceive in your womb and bear a son, and you will name him Jesus. 32He will be great, and will be called the Son of the Most High, and the Lord God will give to him the throne of his ancestor David. 33He will reign over the house of Jacob forever, and of his kingdom there will be no end." 34Mary said to the angel, "How can this be, since I am a virgin?" 35The angel said to her, "The Holy Spirit will come upon you, and the power of the Most High will overshadow you; therefore the child to be born will be holy; he will be called Son of God. 36And now, your relative Elizabeth in her old age has also conceived a son; and this is the sixth month for her who was said to be barren. 37For nothing will be impossible with God." 38Then Mary said, "Here am I, the servant of the Lord; let it be with me according to your word." Then the angel departed from her.*

In three other biblical scenes, a birth is predicted by the proclamation of an angel: the birth of Isaac promised to Abraham and Sarah (Gen 18); the birth of Samson announced to his mother and her husband, Manoah (Judg 13); and the birth of John the Baptist declared to his father, Zechariah (Luke 1). Gabriel's annunciation to Mary is the crown of all the other texts. While this passage contains connections to the other proclamations, the contrasts are more striking. In the other accounts, the couple was barren, unable to have children after a long wait. With Mary, God's intervention was not in response to her yearning for a child nor was it the result of anything she could have anticipated. The text indicates that she is a virgin, and her conception is described as a divine creative action without the normal means of procreation (verses 27, 34). This was unlike anything before in salvation history, as new as God's original creation.

The angel Gabriel greeted Mary with the words: "Greetings, favored one! The Lord is with you" (verse 28). The greeting can also be translated as "hail" or "rejoice," derived from an Old Testament verb expressing joy over a manifestation of God's salvation. The word translated "favored one" is rooted in the Greek word for "grace, favor, blessing, or gift," especially as a manifestation of God's presence. Mary is blessed because God has chosen her for his saving plan. When Mary questions in what way she is graced or favored by God (verse 28–29), the divine grace or favor is confirmed by the angel: "You have found favor with God" (verse 30). Her great favor is the grace of conceiving the Son of God. "The Lord is with you" is an expression of divine assurances throughout the Old Testament at the call of God's servants. As it is used here and as a greeting in Christian liturgy, it is a pledge of God's protective and guiding presence. No matter what obstacles Mary faces, God's plan for her will be realized.

Gabriel's mediation brought Mary into a deep intimacy with God. "The Most High," "the Son of God," and "the Holy Spirit," described in later doctrine as the Trinity, are present here at this climactic moment of saving grace (verse 35). The word of the angel becomes the effective word of God. Mary's child would be the son of David through the human ancestry of his adoptive father Joseph, and Son of God through the divine power overshadowing Mary in this matchless moment of grace.

At the beginning of salvation history, the angel responded to Abraham and Sarah's skepticism about having a child with this timeless question: "Is anything too wonderful for the Lord?" (Gen 18:14). Here at the climax of that saving history, the angel concludes the annunciation to Mary by expressing the trusting confidence urged upon all who receive God's promises: "For nothing will be impossible with God" (verse 37). Mary responds with a total, trusting acceptance of God's gift and humble obedience to God's will: "Let it be with me according to your word" (verse 38). This is the moment of the incarnation of the Son of God. The dialogue between Mary and the angel ceased at once; there was no more for the angel to say or do; he simply departed from her.

Reflectionand discussion

• In what way is the annunciation to Mary the zenith of all other birth announcements in the Bible?

• What in my life has led me to trust in the words of Gabriel: "Nothing will be impossible with God" (verse 37)? What might test those words in the future for me?

Prayer

Son of God and Son of Mary, you came into our world through the powerful will of God and the humble trust of Mary. Help me respond like Mary to the ways you call me to do your will, and let me believe that nothing is impossible with you.

One afternoon at about three o'clock he had a vision in which he clearly saw an angel of God coming in and saying to him, "Cornelius." He stared at him in terror and said, "What is it, Lord?" He answered, "Your prayers and your alms have ascended as a memorial before God." Acts 10:3–4

God's Angel Guides the Church's Mission

ACTS 8:26–31 *²⁶Then an angel of the Lord said to Philip, "Get up and go toward the south to the road that goes down from Jerusalem to Gaza." (This is a wilderness road.) ²⁷So he got up and went. Now there was an Ethiopian eunuch, a court official of the Candace, queen of the Ethiopians, in charge of her entire treasury. He had come to Jerusalem to worship ²⁸and was returning home; seated in his chariot, he was reading the prophet Isaiah. ²⁹Then the Spirit said to Philip, "Go over to this chariot and join it." ³⁰So Philip ran up to it and heard him reading the prophet Isaiah. He asked, "Do you understand what you are reading?" ³¹He replied, "How can I, unless someone guides me?" And he invited Philip to get in and sit beside him.*

ACTS 10:1–8 *¹In Caesarea there was a man named Cornelius, a centurion of the Italian Cohort, as it was called. ²He was a devout man who feared God with all his household; he gave alms generously to the people and prayed constantly to God. ³One afternoon at about three o'clock he had a vision in which he clearly saw an angel of God coming in and saying to him, "Cornelius." ⁴He stared at him in terror and said, "What is it, Lord?" He answered, "Your prayers and your alms have ascended as a memorial before God. ⁵Now send men to Joppa for a certain Simon who is called Peter; ⁶he is lodging with Simon, a tanner, whose house is by the seaside." ⁷When the angel who spoke to him had left, he called two of his slaves and a devout soldier from the ranks of those who served him, ⁸and after telling them everything, he sent them to Joppa.*

The Acts of the Apostles recounts several episodes in which angels assist the new-born church in the missionary spread of the gospel. The disciples of Jesus would have been content to keep the gospel confined within the Jewish community, but it is the nature of the good news of Christ to be ever-expansive into the whole world. So, through the mediation of angels, God moved the early disciples in new and unexpected directions. The Ethiopian court official was probably already a Jewish convert, but the fact that he was from far-away Ethiopia demonstrates how widely the gospel was destined to spread. Cornelius was a Gentile centurion, and his conversion through the ministry of Peter was the first opening of the gospel to non-Jews, a sure indication that there are no boundaries to the spread of the good news of Christ. Being obedient to God's movements, these early missionaries continually find themselves in the oddest of situations with the most surprising sorts of people.

The account of Philip and the Ethiopian begins with the words of "an angel of the Lord." The angel instructs Philip to head toward Gaza along the wilderness road that goes from Jerusalem to Gaza (8:26). Luke introduces the angel in this account to make clear that this mission of Philip is part of God's plan to extend the gospel "to the ends of the earth" (Acts 1:8).

The Ethiopian eunuch was a highly placed official of the Candice, the Ethiopian queen. He was returning to Ethiopia after a pilgrimage to Jerusalem (8:27–28). Ethiopia was included in passages from the Hebrew Scriptures that speak of people from all the nations coming to worship God in Jerusalem. Psalm 68:31 says, "Let Ethiopia hasten to stretch out its hands to God." In the Greco-Roman world the term "Ethiopian" was often applied to black people, those from far-off lands whose dark skin made them an object of wonder and admiration among Jews and Romans.

The Spirit prompted Philip to run up to the chariot of the Ethiopian where the official was reading from a scroll of the prophet Isaiah. It was customary in the ancient world to read aloud, and when Philip heard him reading the words of Israel's prophet, he asked him, "Do you understand what you are reading?"

(8:30). The Ethiopian's response to Philip poses the timeless challenge about the interpretation of Scripture: "How can I, unless someone guides me?" (8:31). One needs guidance to understand the Scriptures properly. The official's invitation to Philip to get in the chariot beside him offers Philip the opportunity to help him understand how the deeper meaning of the passage refers to Christ. The Ethiopian is receptive to Philip's instruction in the Christian faith and asks to be baptized. Though we hear no more of him, we can presume he returned home and spread the good news of Jesus Christ in Ethiopia.

The account of Cornelius, which is a major turning point in the formation of the early church, begins in the city of Caesarea (10:1). Cornelius was a Gentile officer of the Roman army, one who made his living in the military occupation of the Jewish land. Caesarea was the center of the Roman administration of the providence, and the main garrison of its troops, and thus was generally hated by the Jewish people. Yet, for reasons we are not told, Cornelius was attracted to the Jewish religion. "He was a devout man who feared God," and his religious practices included almsgiving and regular prayer (10:2).

At the ninth hour (about three o'clock in the afternoon), the ritual time for Jewish sacrifice and prayer, Cornelius had a vision of an angel which came to him and called out his name (10:3). As is usual with the appearance of an angel, the vision provoked terror in Cornelius, for he felt himself to be in the divine presence. The angel assured Cornelius that his prayers and gifts to the poor had been accepted by God as a sacrificial offering, and then the angel gave him further instructions that would facilitate the next stage in his religious conversion.

The experience of Cornelius, which continues through sixty-six verses, is the longest narrative in Acts and a pivot for the entire book. With the conversion of Cornelius the messianic movement of Jesus' disciples reinterprets itself as a universal and not simply ethnic religion. The narrative involves both Cornelius and Peter, the apostolic spokesman for community, and shuttles back and forth between the two characters. Both have visions; both need divine insight; both need changing if God's mission is to go forward. Peter is led from Joppa to the house of Cornelius in Caesarea. There Peter shares table fellowship with Cornelius and then proclaims the good news of Jesus to his whole household, after which the Holy Spirit came upon them and they are baptized.

These narratives from Acts clearly demonstrate that the mission to spread the gospel is not a human initiative, but the result of the Holy Spirit's impulse and guidance. The message of God's angels and the work of God's Spirit are not separate (compare 8:26 and 8:29). The Holy Spirit is the angel's power and the source of its message. The effect of an angel's message is evidence of God's Spirit at work. As people who continue to be guided by the Holy Spirit, we will be led by God's angels to do things we wouldn't have planned, to meet people we wouldn't have expected to meet. As disciples of Jesus, the initiative for our lives is not our own. Like the people we meet in Acts, we are led by the Spirit of God to do things that are quite beyond our power to initiate or to control.

Reflection and discussion

• Why didn't God just send an angel directly to the Ethiopian, rather than sending the angel to point Philip in the direction of the Ethiopian's travels? What does this tell me about my work in spreading the gospel?

• In what ways does Christian discipleship lead me to surprising people and situations that are beyond my power to initiate or control?

Prayer

Holy Spirit of God, you lead us to places we'd rather not go and to people we'd otherwise not likely meet. Help me realize that as a disciple of Jesus the initiative for my life is not my own. Lead me to where you need me to go in order to be a witness to others of the saving news of Christ.

SUGGESTIONS FOR FACILITATORS, GROUP SESSION 3

1. Welcome group members and ask if there are any announcements anyone would like to make.

2. You may want to pray this prayer as a group:

Lord God, you send your angels as messengers to speak and act on your behalf. Through birth announcements, commissions to leadership, and instructions to your people, you move your saving plan to new stages in human history through the messages of your angels. Send us your angels to inspire new hope within us, to assure us of your presence, to guide us in your will, and to encourage us with the good news of your Son. As we gather to study the angels of the Bible, help us encourage one another and guide us with your Holy Spirit of truth.

3. Ask one or more of the following questions:
   • Which angelic message of this week's readings speaks most powerfully to you?
   • What is the most important lesson you learned through your study this week?

4. Discuss lessons 7 through 12. Choose one or more of the questions for reflection and discussion from each lesson to discuss as a group. You may want to ask group members which question was most challenging or helpful to them as you review each lesson.

5. Remember that there are no definitive answers for these discussion questions. The insights of group members will add to the understanding of all. None of these questions require an expert.

6. After talking about each lesson, instruct group members to complete lessons 13 through 18 on their own during the six days before the next group meeting. They should write out their own answers to the questions as preparation for next week's group discussion.

7. Ask the group if anyone is having any particular problems with the Bible study during the week. You may want to share advice and encouragement within the group.

8. Conclude by praying aloud together the prayer at the end of one of the lessons discussed. You may add to the prayer based on the sharing that has occurred in the group.

For he will command his angels concerning you to guard you in all your ways. On their hands they will bear you up, so that you will not dash your foot against a stone. Ps 91:11–12

Guardians of Those Who Trust in God

PSALM 34:4–10

⁴I sought the Lord, and he answered me,
  and delivered me from all my fears.
⁵Look to him, and be radiant;
  so your faces shall never be ashamed.
⁶This poor soul cried, and was heard by the Lord,
  and was saved from every trouble.
⁷The angel of the Lord encamps
  around those who fear him, and delivers them.
⁸O taste and see that the Lord is good;
  happy are those who take refuge in him.
⁹O fear the Lord, you his holy ones,
  for those who fear him have no want.
¹⁰The young lions suffer want and hunger,
  but those who seek the Lord lack no good thing.

PSALM 91:9–14

[9] *Because you have made the Lord your refuge,*
   the Most High your dwelling place,
[10] *no evil shall befall you,*
   no scourge come near your tent.
[11] *For he will command his angels concerning you*
   to guard you in all your ways.
[12] *On their hands they will bear you up,*
   so that you will not dash your foot against a stone.
[13] *You will tread on the lion and the adder,*
   the young lion and the serpent you will trample under foot.
[14] *Those who love me, I will deliver;*
   I will protect those who know my name.

In addition to their roles as intercessors and messengers of God, angels function as guardians of God's people. God's invisible creation permeates the visible so that we are constantly surrounded by angels who protect and guard us along life's way. Yet, God's protection of each one of us is personal and individual. St. Augustine said, "God is nearer to the soul than it is to itself." Each one of us therefore has been given a guardian angel as an expression and extension of God's personal, attentive care for us.

Psalms 34 and 91 express the poet's experience of God's protection and invite the listener to feel the security of God's care. Those who trust in God as their "refuge" are sheltered from harm (91:9). "Happy are those who take refuge in him" (34:8). They describe the Lord's protection from many different kinds of dangers: hunger, troubles, pestilence, scourge, stumbling, wild animals, and more. This list includes many of the anxieties to which individual life in ancient Israel was subject, yet the dangers are purposely general enough to express the perils that threaten all people. A protective calm from God's presence pervades the poet's words, testifying to the psalmist's long contemplation and quiet spirit of confidence. In past ages, Christians would copy words of these psalms on parchment and wear it as an expression of confidence in God's protection on a journey.

The psalms express the fact that our trust in God is also trust in his protective help exercised through his invisible creation. God protects us from evil and harm through the ministry of his angels. God guards us collectively as his people, his church: "The angel of the Lord encamps around those who fear him, and delivers them" (34:7); God also watches over us individually: "For he will command his angels concerning you, to guard you in all your ways" (91:11). God provides his care for us through them. Just as God sent his angel to guard his people on their journey through the desert (Exod 23:20; 32:34; 33:2), God orders his angels to protect us along the journey of life, lifting us up with their hands lest we stumble along the way (91:12). The pitfalls along our journey may be physical or spiritual. In either case, God is our protector as he sends his angels to be our escorts and guards.

For some, Psalm 91 provides some of the most comforting promises in the Bible. For others, these promises are some of the most unrealistic. What about those who have experienced tragedy? Don't these comforting assurances seem even cruel? Because the assurance of security in this psalm is so comprehensive and confident, it is especially subject to misuse and to that ever-present temptation to turn faith into superstition. Satan himself exploited the words about God's angels in order to tempt Jesus to throw himself down from the pinnacle of the temple: "He will command his angels concerning you, to protect you" (Ps 91:11–12; Matt 4:5–7; Luke 4:10–11). Jesus saw Satan's use of the psalm as an inexcusable way to test God, not as the way of trust. Genuine trust does not seek to test God or to prove his faithfulness. As shown by the life of Jesus, God does not promise us immunization from trouble. God's protection, rather, assures us of God's intimate concern for each of us and of the ability to know God's presence in the midst of trials so that we will be strengthened and purified along life's way.

Reflection and discussion

• In what ways have I experienced God's personal protection and watchful care?

• What is the difference between testing God and trusting God? How do these psalms help me understand the difference?

• How are the perils that I face in life similiar to the dangers mentioned by the psalmists?

• Which verse of these psalms would I most like to remember along life's journey? In what way do these words give me inspiration or security?

Prayer

God Most High, you are my refuge and my fortress. Thank you for delivering me from fear and protecting me from evil. Send your angels to lift me up from dangers and guide me along life's journey.

The angel of the Lord said to her, "Now you have conceived and shall bear a son; you shall call him Ishmael, for the Lord has given heed to your affliction."

Gen 16:11

Rescuing the Beloved of Abraham

GENESIS 16:1– 16 *¹Now Sarai, Abram's wife, bore him no children. She had an Egyptian slave-girl whose name was Hagar, ²and Sarai said to Abram, "You see that the Lord has prevented me from bearing children; go in to my slave-girl; it may be that I shall obtain children by her." And Abram listened to the voice of Sarai. ³So, after Abram had lived ten years in the land of Canaan, Sarai, Abram's wife, took Hagar the Egyptian, her slave-girl, and gave her to her husband Abram as a wife. ⁴He went in to Hagar, and she conceived; and when she saw that she had conceived, she looked with contempt on her mistress. ⁵Then Sarai said to Abram, "May the wrong done to me be on you! I gave my slave-girl to your embrace, and when she saw that she had conceived, she looked on me with contempt. May the Lord judge between you and me!" ⁶But Abram said to Sarai, "Your slave-girl is in your power; do to her as you please." Then Sarai dealt harshly with her, and she ran away from her.*

⁷The angel of the Lord found her by a spring of water in the wilderness, the spring on the way to Shur. ⁸And he said, "Hagar, slave-girl of Sarai, where have you come from and where are you going?" She said, "I am running away from my mistress Sarai." ⁹The angel of the Lord said to her, "Return to your mistress, and submit to her." ¹⁰The angel of the Lord also said to her, "I will so greatly mul-

tiply your offspring that they cannot be counted for multitude." [11]*And the angel of the Lord said to her,*

> *"Now you have conceived and shall bear a son;*
>> *you shall call him Ishmael,*
>> *for the Lord has given heed to your affliction.*
> [12]*He shall be a wild ass of a man,*
> *with his hand against everyone,*
>> *and everyone's hand against him;*
> *and he shall live at odds with all his kin."*

[13]*So she named the Lord who spoke to her, "You are El-roi"; for she said, "Have I really seen God and remained alive after seeing him?"* [14]*Therefore the well was called Beer-lahai-roi; it lies between Kadesh and Bered.*

[15]*Hagar bore Abram a son; and Abram named his son, whom Hagar bore, Ishmael.* [16]*Abram was eighty-six years old when Hagar bore him Ishmael.*

GENESIS 22:9–14 [9]*When they came to the place that God had shown him, Abraham built an altar there and laid the wood in order. He bound his son Isaac, and laid him on the altar, on top of the wood.* [10]*Then Abraham reached out his hand and took the knife to kill his son.* [11]*But the angel of the Lord called to him from heaven, and said, "Abraham, Abraham!" And he said, "Here I am."* [12]*He said, "Do not lay your hand on the boy or do anything to him; for now I know that you fear God, since you have not withheld your son, your only son, from me."* [13]*And Abraham looked up and saw a ram, caught in a thicket by its horns. Abraham went and took the ram and offered it up as a burnt offering instead of his son.* [14]*So Abraham called that place "The Lord will provide"; as it is said to this day, "On the mount of the Lord it shall be provided."*

Unable to conceive a child after many years, Sarai had provided her husband with a concubine in order to bear a child. Hagar, Sarai's Egyptian maidservant, conceived a child by Abram, but Sarai's resentment and jealousy grew so strong that Hagar ran away into the desert. Here in the wilderness, as Hagar is fleeing back to her native land, we are presented with the Bible's first appearance of an angel as a messenger of God.

God, the guardian of the weak and downtrodden, has chosen to reveal himself to this outcast servant through his angel. God has seen her fear and desolation, and has decided to intervene. That God would choose Hagar as the first person in salvation history to whom he sent an angel is remarkable. Hagar is a woman, an Egyptian, and a slave, all inferior positions in the ancient Israelite culture in which this account was written. In addition, her future son Ishmael and his descendants will live in conflict with the Israelites. Yet, the angel of the Lord sought out Hagar and found her by a spring of water, at an oasis in the desert, in order to bring her a message of comfort and hope (16:7).

It seems that all parties, Abraham, Sarah, and Hagar, would have left well enough alone had not God chosen to intervene. God reopens the issue and offers Hagar new strength and direction. The angel tells her to return the way she has come and to submit to her mistress Sarai (16:9). In this way her son Ishmael will be raised in the household of Abraham as his son. Then, echoing God's promise to Abram, the angel tells Hagar that her offspring will be innumerable (16:10). Her son is to be called Ishmael, a name which means "God hears," for as the angel proclaimed, "The Lord has given heed to your affliction" (16:11).

The significance of Ishmael's name will become clearer many years later when Hagar once again flees from Sarai's jealousy, this time with her adolescent son. Dying of thirst in the wilderness, God hears the boy's crying and the angel of God called to Hagar from heaven and said, "Do not be afraid; for God has heard the voice of the boy where he is" (21:17). The angel then confirms Ishmael's destiny: "Come, lift up the boy and hold him fast with your hand, for I will make a great nation of him" (21:18).

The angel reveals to Hagar in both encounters the purposeful compassion of God. Yet, already in the first angelic encounter of the Bible, there is no clear distinction between the appearance and voice of God and that of God's angel. After the message of the angel is given, Hagar wonders in amazement, "Have I really seen God and remained alive after seeing him?" (16:13). Awed by this divine encounter, Hagar becomes the only person in the Bible to give a name to God: "You are El-roi." The name is wonderfully ambiguous, allowing it several translations simultaneously: "God of seeing," that is, the all-seeing God; "God of my seeing," that is, whom I have seen; and "God who sees me." When God sees, as Hagar has discovered, he extends his protection and shows his loving care; when Hagar sees, she experiences God's self-manifestation.

This protective care manifested through God's angel is also shown to Abraham on the momentous occasion in which he is called to sacrifice his other son, Isaac, the son of the promise (22:9). In obedience Abraham took him to the mountain and tied him to the wood on the altar of sacrifice. Just as Abraham raised his knife to slay his son, the angel of the Lord called to him from heaven (22:11). Calling Abraham's name, the angel said to him, "Do not lay your hand on the boy or do anything to him; for now I know that you fear God, since you have not withheld your son, your only son, from me" (22:12). The angel then confirmed God's promise to Abraham that his offspring would be as numerous as the stars of the sky and the sand on the seashore (22:17).

In both of these life-threatening trials—the first with Abraham's elder son Ishmael and then with his younger son Isaac—the angel calls at the decisive moment and rescues. Calling out first to a frantic mother and then to an agonizing father, the angel protects the child from death and then unfolds a future in which each child will beget countless descendants. Both narratives reveal God's unfailing love and reveal God's angel as a guardian who enables God's people to trust.

Reflection and discussion

• Why does God wait until the moment of desperation in these accounts before he sends his angel?

• In what ways do these accounts show me God's protective care? In what ways do they instill trust within me?

Prayer

God of Vision, I have seen you in the biblical narratives and in the experiences of my life. You see the needs of your people and rescue them in desperate times. Help me open my eyes to those around me so that I can see their needs and their pains.

"My God sent his angel and shut the lions' mouths so that they would not hurt me, because I was found blameless before him; and also before you, O king, I have done no wrong." Dan 6:22

Deliverance from the Jaws of Death

DANIEL 3:16–23, 46–50, 91–95 *¹⁶Shadrach, Meshach, and Abednego answered the king, "O Nebuchadnezzar, we have no need to present a defense to you in this matter. ¹⁷If our God whom we serve is able to deliver us from the furnace of blazing fire and out of your hand, O king, let him deliver us. ¹⁸But if not, be it known to you, O king, that we will not serve your gods and we will not worship the golden statue that you have set up."*

¹⁹Then Nebuchadnezzar was so filled with rage against Shadrach, Meshach, and Abednego that his face was distorted. He ordered the furnace heated up seven times more than was customary, ²⁰and ordered some of the strongest guards in his army to bind Shadrach, Meshach, and Abednego and to throw them into the furnace of blazing fire. ²¹So the men were bound, still wearing their tunics, their trousers, their hats, and their other garments, and they were thrown into the furnace of blazing fire. ²²Because the king's command was urgent and the furnace was so overheated, the raging flames killed the men who lifted Shadrach, Meshach, and Abednego. ²³But the three men, Shadrach, Meshach, and Abednego, fell down, bound, into the furnace of blazing fire.

⁴⁶Now the king's servants who threw them in kept stoking the furnace with naphtha, pitch, tow, and brushwood. ⁴⁷And the flames poured out above the fur-

nace forty-nine cubits, [48]and spread out and burned those Chaldeans who were caught near the furnace. [49]But the angel of the Lord came down into the furnace to be with Azariah [Abednego] and his companions, and drove the fiery flame out of the furnace, [50]and made the inside of the furnace as though a moist wind were whistling through it. The fire did not touch them at all and caused them no pain or distress.

[91]Then King Nebuchadnezzar was astonished and rose up quickly. He said to his counselors, "Was it not three men that we threw bound into the fire?" They answered the king, "True, O king." [92]He replied, "But I see four men unbound, walking in the middle of the fire, and they are not hurt; and the fourth has the appearance of a god." [93]Nebuchadnezzar then approached the door of the furnace of blazing fire and said, "Shadrach, Meshach, and Abednego, servants of the Most High God, come out! Come here!" So Shadrach, Meshach, and Abednego came out from the fire. [94]And the satraps, the prefects, the governors, and the king's counselors gathered together and saw that the fire had not had any power over the bodies of those men; the hair of their heads was not singed, their tunics were not harmed, and not even the smell of fire came from them. [95]Nebuchadnezzar said, "Blessed be the God of Shadrach, Meshach, and Abednego, who has sent his angel and delivered his servants who trusted in him. They disobeyed the king's command and yielded up their bodies rather than serve and worship any god except their own God.

DANIEL 6:16–23 [16]Then the king gave the command, and Daniel was brought and thrown into the den of lions. The king said to Daniel, "May your God, whom you faithfully serve, deliver you!" [17]A stone was brought and laid on the mouth of the den, and the king sealed it with his own signet and with the signet of his lords, so that nothing might be changed concerning Daniel. [18]Then the king went to his palace and spent the night fasting; no food was brought to him, and sleep fled from him.

[19]Then, at break of day, the king got up and hurried to the den of lions. [20]When he came near the den where Daniel was, he cried out anxiously to Daniel, "O Daniel, servant of the living God, has your God whom you faithfully serve been able to deliver you from the lions?" [21]Daniel then said to the king, "O king, live forever! [22]My God sent his angel and shut the lions' mouths so that they would not hurt me, because I was found blameless before him; and also before you, O king, I have done no wrong." [23]Then the king was exceedingly glad and commanded

that Daniel be taken up out of the den. So Daniel was taken up out of the den,
and no kind of harm was found on him, because he had trusted in his God.

These two stories from the book of Daniel are set in Babylon where the
Jewish people often experienced jealous resentment and religious persecution. The question in each of these accounts is whether or not
God will deliver his faithful ones from harm. The narratives of the three
young men thrown into the fiery furnace and Daniel thrown into the pit of
lions each present an extraordinary danger and a remarkable, unexpected
deliverance. In both stories, God's deliverance is mediated by an angel.

When King Nebuchadnezzar commanded all his subjects to worship a
colossal golden statue, he threatened the young Jewish men, Shadrach,
Meshach, and Abednego with death in a fiery furnace for refusing to do so.
The young heroes utterly refuse to participate in idolatry. They are motivat-
ed not by an absolute confidence that God will save them from such an
impossible situation, but by absolute clarity about what God expects in this
situation. In their statement of loyalty the three young men have already
defeated their oppressor (3:17–18).

After the three companions had been bound and thrown into the fire and
the furnace had been heated up far beyond its normal intensity, the angel of
the Lord came down into the furnace to be with the young men. The story
says that the angel "drove the fiery flame out of the furnace, and made the
inside of the furnace as though a moist wind were whistling through it"
(3:49–50). King Nebuchadnezzar relates his astonishment: "I see four men
unbound, walking in the middle of the fire, and they are not hurt; and the
fourth has the appearance of a god" (3:92). When the king ordered the youths
to come out of the furnace, the king and his counselors saw that the fire had
done absolutely no harm to them. The king praised God saying, "Blessed be
the God of Shadrach, Meshach, and Abednego, who has sent his angel and
delivered his servants who trusted in him" (3:95).

Some time after this event, the next king, Darius, placed Daniel over all his
governors. Jealous of Daniel's success, the governors plotted Daniel's down-
fall. They manipulated King Darius to sign a decree stating that anyone who
prayed to another besides King Darius shall be thrown into a den of lions.
Daniel quietly disobeyed the order, praying three times a day from his room
in the direction of Jerusalem. Like the three young men, Daniel knew what he

must do in the face of a human law that contradicts the law of God. When the governors reported Daniel's dissent to the king, Darius reluctantly ordered that Daniel be thrown into the den of lions. Unable to change his own law, the king uttered this enigmatic wish to Daniel: "May your God, whom you faithfully serve, deliver you!" (6:16).

The king himself sealed the exit of the lion's den with a large stone and spent the night in fasting. At daybreak, the king hurried to the lion's den, hoping against hope, knowing that deliverance from such an impossible situation could be accomplished only by the living God (6:20). Daniel, unharmed, reports the miraculous intervention of an angel: "My God sent his angel and shut the lions' mouth so that they would not hurt me" (6:22).

In both of these accounts, God has indeed delivered his servants who trust in him. The divine nature of their delivery is emphasized by statements that the heroes are completely unharmed. The three young men are saved so completely from harm that the hair of their head was not singed and they didn't even have the smell of fire on their tunics (3:94). Daniel emerged from the den of lions and upon examination by the king "no kind of harm was found on him" (6:23). Deliverance from the fiery furnace and deliverance from the lion's mouth are powerful religious metaphors for deliverance from any desperate situation. There is always room for hope for those who trust in God. The temporal powers that threaten God's faithful ones are not permanent. The one power that ultimately directs the world and human history is the power of the living God who will ultimately deliver his people from all that threatens them.

Reflection and discussion

• In what ways do these two stories help me to trust in the face of danger?

• In what way is the response of the three young men already a defeat of their oppressor (3:17–18)?

• What is my responsibility when faced with a human decree that contradicts the law of God? Have I ever been faced with such a dilemma?

• In what way have I experienced deliverance in a desperate situation? How can I trust more fully in God's deliverance from all that threatens me?

Prayer

Living God, you deliver your people from threat and danger, and you promise to save us from all that separates us from you. Give me the gift of confident trust and let me turn to you in the face of life's perils and threats.

"I am Raphael, one of the seven angels who stand ready and enter before the glory of the Lord." Tob 12:15

Raphael Reveals God's Guiding Presence

TOBIT 12:1–22 ¹*When the wedding celebration was ended, Tobit called his son Tobias and said to him, "My child, see to paying the wages of the man who went with you, and give him a bonus as well." ²He replied, "Father, how much shall I pay him? It would do no harm to give him half of the possessions brought back with me. ³For he has led me back to you safely, he cured my wife, he brought the money back with me, and he healed you. How much extra shall I give him as a bonus?" ⁴Tobit said, "He deserves, my child, to receive half of all that he brought back." ⁵So Tobias called him and said, "Take for your wages half of all that you brought back, and farewell."*

⁶*Then Raphael called the two of them privately and said to them, "Bless God and acknowledge him in the presence of all the living for the good things he has done for you. Bless and sing praise to his name. With fitting honor declare to all people the deeds of God. Do not be slow to acknowledge him. ⁷It is good to conceal the secret of a king, but to acknowledge and reveal the works of God, and with fitting honor to acknowledge him. Do good and evil will not overtake you. ⁸Prayer with fasting is good, but better than both is almsgiving with righteousness. A little with righteousness is better than wealth with wrongdoing. It is better to give alms than to lay up gold. ⁹For almsgiving saves from death and purges away every sin. Those who give alms will enjoy a full life, ¹⁰but those who commit sin and do wrong are their own worst enemies.*

¹¹ *"I will now declare the whole truth to you and will conceal nothing from you. Already I have declared it to you when I said, 'It is good to conceal the secret of a king, but to reveal with due honor the works of God.'* ¹² *So now when you and Sarah prayed, it was I who brought and read the record of your prayer before the glory of the Lord, and likewise whenever you would bury the dead.* ¹³ *And that time when you did not hesitate to get up and leave your dinner to go and bury the dead,* ¹⁴ *I was sent to you to test you. And at the same time God sent me to heal you and Sarah your daughter-in-law.* ¹⁵ *I am Raphael, one of the seven angels who stand ready and enter before the glory of the Lord."*

¹⁶ *The two of them were shaken; they fell face down, for they were afraid.* ¹⁷ *But he said to them, "Do not be afraid; peace be with you. Bless God forevermore.* ¹⁸ *As for me, when I was with you, I was not acting on my own will, but by the will of God. Bless him each and every day; sing his praises.* ¹⁹ *Although you were watching me, I really did not eat or drink anything—but what you saw was a vision.* ²⁰ *So now get up from the ground, and acknowledge God. See, I am ascending to him who sent me. Write down all these things that have happened to you." And he ascended.* ²¹ *Then they stood up, and could see him no more.* ²² *They kept blessing God and singing his praises, and they acknowledged God for these marvelous deeds of his, when an angel of God had appeared to them.*

Tobit is a charming story about two Jewish families living in exile in foreign lands. Tobit and Sarah are both righteous people who are unexplainably smitten by misfortune. Tobit has been reduced to poverty and afflicted with blindness. Sarah has lost seven husbands, all of them killed on their wedding night. The story weaves these two families together and becomes a lesson on how to live faithfully in covenant while away from the land of Israel.

Recalling a large sum of money he had deposited in far off Media, Tobit sends his son Tobias on a long journey to bring back the money. Tobias is accompanied by the angel Raphael, though Tobias does not realize that his companion is an angel (see chapters 5–6). Raphael appears convincingly human to the characters within the story, yet he performs multiple angelic roles in the story, as he guards, guides, defeats evil, and heals. The angel saves Tobias from danger, brings about his marriage to Sarah, and brings him back home with the money and with a cure for Tobit's blindness (verse 3). The work of Raphael convinces us that God is always with his people: in their sufferings and their fears, in their love and their celebrations, in their homes and on their travels.

At the end of this long adventure culminating in a wedding, Raphael finally reveals himself as an angel: "I am Raphael, one of the seven angels who stand ready and enter before the glory of the Lord" (verse 15). He discloses that when Tobit and Sarah prayed, he brought their prayers before the glory of God (verse 12). He also admits that he is the one God sent to heal Tobit and Sarah (verse 14). Yet, rather than bringing glory to himself, Raphael urges his listeners to acknowledge God's work and to bless and sing praise to God's name (verses 6–7, 18–22). Finally, Raphael ascends and returns to heaven, ready again to do God's bidding the lives of his people on earth. Raphael reveals God's constant presence and interest, and exemplifies the ministry of God's angels in the great and small affairs of human life.

Reflection and discussion

• What are some of Raphael's multiple roles in this story? What does this indicate about the ways God is present in my daily life?

• Why did Raphael not reveal his true nature until the end of the story? What does his disguise teach me about the ways of God's angels?

• Why does Raphael insist that it is good to acknowledge the works of God (verses 7, 11)? How can I give God greater honor for his works in my life?

• What other angelic advice does Raphael offer to his earthly charges?

• What questions does this story raise for me about the work of God's angels?

Prayer

Blessed are you, God of our ancestors, and blessed is your name in all generations for ever. Have compassion upon me, and deal with me according to your great mercy. Bring my life to fulfillment in happiness and in peace.

"Take care that you do not despise one of these little ones; for, I tell you, in heaven their angels continually see the face of my Father in heaven." Matt 18:10

Guardian Angels Care for God's Little Ones

MATTHEW 18:1–14 *¹At that time the disciples came to Jesus and asked, "Who is the greatest in the kingdom of heaven?" ²He called a child, whom he put among them, ³and said, "Truly I tell you, unless you change and become like children, you will never enter the kingdom of heaven. ⁴Whoever becomes humble like this child is the greatest in the kingdom of heaven. ⁵Whoever welcomes one such child in my name welcomes me.*

⁶"If any of you put a stumbling block before one of these little ones who believe in me, it would be better for you if a great millstone were fastened around your neck and you were drowned in the depth of the sea. ⁷Woe to the world because of stumbling blocks! Occasions for stumbling are bound to come, but woe to the one by whom the stumbling block comes!

⁸"If your hand or your foot causes you to stumble, cut it off and throw it away; it is better for you to enter life maimed or lame than to have two hands or two feet and to be thrown into the eternal fire. ⁹And if your eye causes you to stumble, tear it out and throw it away; it is better for you to enter life with one eye than to have two eyes and to be thrown into the hell of fire.

¹⁰"Take care that you do not despise one of these little ones; for, I tell you, in heaven their angels continually see the face of my Father in heaven.¹² What do you think? If a shepherd has a hundred sheep, and one of them has gone astray,

does he not leave the ninety-nine on the mountains and go in search of the one
that went astray? [13] *And if he finds it, truly I tell you, he rejoices over it more than*
over the ninety-nine that never went astray. [14] *So it is not the will of your Father*
in heaven that one of these little ones should be lost.

T he Christian understanding of guardian angels grew out of the teachings of Jesus concerning the individual protective care that God has
for each and every person. God's care of his people is so individual-
ized that he cannot bear the loss of even one person. God is like the shepherd
who would leave all the other sheep of his flock to go after a single sheep who
had gone astray. That one individual sheep is more important to the shepherd
at that moment than all the others, and when the shepherd finds the lost one
he rejoices over its finding (verses 12–14). Jesus urges this type of pastoral
care from those who would shepherd his church. They cannot simply care
about crowds of people, but they must care about each individual because
each one is infinitely valuable to God.

When Jesus was teaching his disciples about the qualities necessary for
entry into the kingdom of heaven, he called a child into their midst. "Unless
you change and become like children, you will never enter the kingdom of
heaven," he said (verse 3). Jesus is recommending not childishness but a
child-like trust in a loving Father. We love to give children gifts because they
know they don't have to earn them. Only those who receive God's grace in
this way can fully respond to it. We enter God's kingdom with confident
humility, awaiting everything and grabbing at nothing (verse 4).

This discourse of Jesus makes a transition from children to those who take on
the trusting and humble disposition of children. These are, in the words of Jesus,
"the little ones who believe in me" (verse 6). Jesus urges his followers to take
great care with the trusting faith of these little ones, and he warns that anyone
who puts a "stumbling block" (scandal) before one of these little ones will suffer serious consequences. Simple trust in another person is a beautiful but frag-
ile relationship that can be shattered with a single offense. Jesus makes it clear
that nothing is worse than betraying the humble confidence of a new believer.

Jesus gives a further reason to treat God's little ones with great care: their
guardian angels have direct access to the divine presence. "Take care that you
do not despise one of these little ones," Jesus says, "for, I tell you, in heaven
their angels continually see the face of my Father in heaven" (verse 10). Some

strains of first-century Judaism had developed teachings about individual guardian angels assigned to each person by God. But this Jewish teaching also held that only the highest of angels could see God's face, that is, have direct access to the divine presence. Jesus establishes that the angels who watch over God's little ones and plead their cause before God have the highest status. Thus God's little ones, those of simple and humble faith, have the highest importance. Thus no believer, no matter how marginal or insignificant in the world, is to be treated as inferior in the Christian community, because even the lowliest Christian has a guardian angel who is an "angel of the presence."

Reflection and discussion

• In what way does Jesus' saying about guardian angels and his parable of the shepherd contain the same message? What do they tell me about God's care?

• Why does Jesus urge us to become like children? How can I become more like a child in order to enter the kingdom of heaven?

Prayer

Father in heaven, you create every person with infinite value in your eyes. Watch over us as the shepherd guards the sheep and send your angels to guide us along life's way. Give me a childlike trust in you so that I can respond fully to your grace.

Suddenly an angel of the Lord appeared and a light shone in the cell. He tapped Peter on the side and woke him, saying, "Get up quickly." And the chains fell off his wrists. Acts 12:7

Peter Is Rescued from Prison

ACTS 12:1–17 *¹About that time King Herod laid violent hands upon some who belonged to the church. ²He had James, the brother of John, killed with the sword. ³After he saw that it pleased the Jews, he proceeded to arrest Peter also. (This was during the festival of Unleavened Bread.) ⁴When he had seized him, he put him in prison and handed him over to four squads of soldiers to guard him, intending to bring him out to the people after the Passover. ⁵While Peter was kept in prison, the church prayed fervently to God for him.*

⁶The very night before Herod was going to bring him out, Peter, bound with two chains, was sleeping between two soldiers, while guards in front of the door were keeping watch over the prison. ⁷Suddenly an angel of the Lord appeared and a light shone in the cell. He tapped Peter on the side and woke him, saying, "Get up quickly." And the chains fell off his wrists. ⁸The angel said to him, "Fasten your belt and put on your sandals." He did so. Then he said to him, "Wrap your cloak around you and follow me." ⁹Peter went out and followed him; he did not realize that what was happening with the angel's help was real; he thought he was seeing a vision. ¹⁰After they had passed the first and the second guard, they came before the iron gate leading into the city. It opened for them of its own accord, and they went outside and walked along a lane, when suddenly the angel left him. ¹¹Then Peter came to himself and said, "Now I am sure that the Lord has sent his angel and rescued me from the hands of Herod and from all that the Jewish people were expecting."

¹²As soon as he realized this, he went to the house of Mary, the mother of John whose other name was Mark, where many had gathered and were praying. ¹³When he knocked at the outer gate, a maid named Rhoda came to answer. ¹⁴On recognizing Peter's voice, she was so overjoyed that, instead of opening the gate, she ran in and announced that Peter was standing at the gate. ¹⁵They said to her, "You are out of your mind!" But she insisted that it was so. They said, "It is his angel." ¹⁶Meanwhile Peter continued knocking; and when they opened the gate, they saw him and were amazed. ¹⁷He motioned to them with his hand to be silent, and described for them how the Lord had brought him out of the prison. And he added, "Tell this to James and to the believers." Then he left and went to another place.

God's rescue of Peter through the ministry of an angel is a result of God's guiding care for his church and the prayers of the faithful community. King Herod, who had been persecuting the church and putting its leaders to death, has now arrested and imprisoned Peter. His intention was to bring him out for trial and public execution immediately after the celebration of Passover (verses 1–4). But knowing how many public and secret sympathizers the apostles had in Jerusalem, Herod had taken every precaution against any attempt to free his prisoner. The four squads of soldiers took turns guarding Peter during the four watches of the night, with each watch of three hours being kept by four soldiers. The usual security required that two should guard the prisoner within the cell, chained to him one on each side, and that two should be outside guarding the doors (verse 6). Though Peter's situation looked hopeless, "the church prayed fervently to God for him" (verse 5). The power of the church is the power of prayer, a seemingly impotent force in the face of Herod's prison, chains, soldiers, and guards.

But into the bleak darkness of Peter's prison cell fell the light of God's saving power. "Suddenly an angel of the Lord appeared and a light shone in the cell" (verse 7). As the angel woke Peter from sleep, the events of Peter's rescue occurred in rapid succession. The chains by which he was handcuffed to the soldiers on either side fell as he got up. The angel ordered him to fasten his belt, tie on his sandals, wrap his cloak around him, and follow (verse 8).

Peter did as he was told, only half-awake, not realizing what was really happening, thinking that he would soon awake from a dream. They passed through one gate and then another, both of them guarded. The final obstacle, the iron gate leading into the city, opened spontaneously as they approached, and they found themselves walking along the streets of the city (verses 9–10). With the release complete, the angel departed. Fully awake and aware of his new freedom, Peter was quick to recognize the hand of the Lord in his deliverance: "Now I am sure that the Lord has sent his angel and rescued me" (verse 11).

Because the church in Jerusalem was too large to gather in any one place, it was divided into a number of house churches where its members met for worship and fellowship. When Peter arrived at the house, he knocked at the gate of the courtyard and the housemaid named Rhoda answered. She was so excited to hear Peter's voice that she forgot to let him in (verses 12–14). When she ran inside to tell the others, they could not believe that their prayers had been answered so quickly or that Peter had escaped from such an impossible bondage. "It is his angel," they speculated (verse 15). This refers to the popular belief at the time that a guardian angel was so closely associated with the person guarded that it was capable of assuming his voice and bodily appearance. The playful humor in this account is hard to miss. An angel escorts Peter through the iron gate of Herod's prison, but Peter himself cannot get through the locked gate of the Christian household because they mistake him for an angel. Finally, after Peter continued knocking, the crowd went to find out who's there by the practical expedient of opening the gate. Then motioning with his hand to silence the excited gathering, Peter related all the details of his miraculous rescue.

Reflection and discussion

• What worldly forces seem all-powerful to me? How does this narrative put them in perspective?

• Why did God save Peter and not James (verses 2–3)? Why does God rescue some and not others?

• From what prison or bondage do I need God's rescue? How trusting am I of God's power to deliver me?

• Do I trust in the effectiveness of prayer? Do I believe that the power of the church is the power of prayer?

Prayer

Lord Jesus Christ, you rose from the dark bondage of the tomb and empowered your church to experience liberation from all bondage. Free me from the chains that bind me so that I can witness your power in my life.

SUGGESTIONS FOR FACILITATORS, GROUP SESSION 4

1. Welcome group members and ask if anyone has any questions, announcements, or requests.

2. You may want to pray this prayer as a group:

Lord God, you protect your people from danger and you care about the life and salvation of every person. You sent your angels to release Hagar, Ishmael, Isaac, Daniel, and Peter from peril, bondage, and death, and through the ministry of your guardian angels, you guide us, protect us, rescue us, and shield us from harm. As we gather together with many hungers, uncertainties, and fears, give us a deep trust in you and command your angels to guard, defend, and deliver us from every evil.

3. Ask one or more of the following questions:
   • What is the most difficult part of this study for you?
   • What insights stands out to you from the lessons this week?

4. Discuss lessons 13 through 18. Choose one or more of the questions for reflection and discussion from each lesson to discuss as a group. You may want to ask group members which question was most challenging or helpful to them as you review each lesson.

5. Keep the discussion moving, but allow time for the questions that provoke the most discussion. Encourage the group members to use "I" language in their responses.

6. After talking over each lesson, instruct group members to complete lessons 19 through 24 on their own during the six days before the next group meeting. They should write out their own answers to the questions as preparation for next week's session.

7. Ask the group what encouragement they need for the coming week. Ask the members to pray for the needs of one another during the week.

8. Conclude by praying aloud together the prayer at the end of one of the lessons discussed. You may choose to conclude the prayer by asking members to pray aloud for any requests they may have.

When the devil had finished every test, he departed from him until an opportune time. Luke 4:13

Jesus Is Tempted by the Devil

MATTHEW 4:1–11 *¹Then Jesus was led up by the Spirit into the wilderness to be tempted by the devil. ²He fasted forty days and forty nights, and afterwards he was famished. ³The tempter came and said to him, "If you are the Son of God, command these stones to become loaves of bread." ⁴But he answered, "It is written,*

> *'One does not live by bread alone,*
>> *but by every word that comes from the mouth of God.'"*

⁵Then the devil took him to the holy city and placed him on the pinnacle of the temple, ⁶saying to him, "If you are the Son of God, throw yourself down; for it is written,

> *'He will command his angels concerning you,'*
>> *and 'On their hands they will bear you up,*
>>> *so that you will not dash your foot against a stone.'"*

⁷Jesus said to him, "Again it is written, 'Do not put the Lord your God to the test.'"

⁸Again, the devil took him to a very high mountain and showed him all the kingdoms of the world and their splendor; ⁹and he said to him, "All these I will give you, if you will fall down and worship me." ¹⁰Jesus said to him, "Away with you, Satan! for it is written,

'Worship the Lord your God,
and serve only him.'"

¹¹ Then the devil left him, and suddenly angels came and waited on him.

LUKE 22:39–46 ³⁹ He came out and went, as was his custom, to the Mount
of Olives; and the disciples followed him. ⁴⁰ When he reached the place, he said to
them, "Pray that you may not come into the time of trial." ⁴¹ Then he withdrew
from them about a stone's throw, knelt down, and prayed, ⁴² "Father, if you are
willing, remove this cup from me; yet, not my will but yours be done." ⁴³ Then an
angel from heaven appeared to him and gave him strength. ⁴⁴ In his anguish he
prayed more earnestly, and his sweat became like great drops of blood falling
down on the ground. ⁴⁵ When he got up from prayer, he came to the disciples and
found them sleeping because of grief, ⁴⁶ and he said to them, "Why are you sleeping? Get up and pray that you may not come into the time of trial."

While we are amazed at the wondrous power of God's angels in
mediating God's presence and expressing God's will for humanity, we must also look at the negative side of a study of angels.
Though all of God's creation, including the angels, was originally good, both
angels and humans were given the ability to freely choose how they would
respond to their creator (2 Peter 2:4). When some of the angels chose to rebel
against God, irrevocably rejecting God and his reign, they became adversaries
of God's kingdom, tempting humanity to rebellious opposition to God's loving plan. Though their diabolical activity is allowed for a time under God's
mysterious providence, their power is not infinite or equal to God's, and at
some future time they will be permanently restrained and vanquished.

The figure of "Satan" or "the devil" occurs frequently in the New
Testament. *Satan* in Hebrew and *diabolos* in Greek is an adversary, accuser, or
plotter. The figure in the Bible describes a supernatural being who is the
adversary of God's people, striving mightily to divert them from the path of
obedience to God's caring design and to break their bond with God. The
devil's main instrument for this work is a "test" of people's trust in God and
faithfulness to his will. This testing is usually translated as "temptation," but
more accurately as "trial."

Being tested by the devil is not an indication of weakness, but of strength.
The greater the strength, the greater the temptation. Thus the greatest trial

ever imposed by Satan was the testing he inflicted on Jesus from the beginning of his public ministry in the wilderness to the end on the Mount of Olives and the hill of Calvary. The concern of the narrative is not so much whether the devil can lure Jesus into specific sins as it is the depiction of Jesus as the Son of God "who in every respect has been tested as we are, yet without sin" (Heb 4:15). In the wilderness, where no one can observe and where the heart is laid bare, Jesus chooses not the lures of personal pleasure, possessions, and glory, but the will of God that directed his saving mission.

At the conclusion of the testing, in Matthew's gospel, Jesus sent Satan packing, "Away with you, Satan!" and the devil left him, and angels came and served him (Matt 4:10–11). In Luke's version, the ending is far more foreboding: "When the devil had finished every test, he departed from him until an opportune time" (Luke 4:13). The tempter will watch and wait for a more favorable opportunity. That time of trial is experienced most intensely during the passion of Jesus.

When Jesus came to the Mount of Olives, one of his apostles had already failed the testing: "Satan entered into Judas called Iscariot" (Luke 22:3). The others were entering a time of fierce temptation. Jesus said to Peter, "Satan has demanded to sift all of you like wheat, but I have prayed for you that your own faith may not fail" (Luke 22:31). When they entered the place called Gethsemane, Jesus urged his disciples, "Pray that you may not come into the time of trial" (Luke 22:40, 46). Then Jesus himself entered an intense struggle with the power of darkness, while an angel from heaven appeared to give him strength (Luke 22:43). In anguish he prayed as his sweat fell like globules of blood, foreshadowing the even harder trial the next day when he would shed his blood on the cross.

Reflection and discussion

• What from these narratives helps me in my own struggle with the powers of evil?

• How did some of God's angels become adversaries of God and humanity?

• What is the test that I most often fail? What is the test that proves my fidelity?

• Why is it important for me to know that Jesus was tested in every way we are? How can I best imitate Jesus during my own times of testing and trial?

Prayer

Son of God, you battled with the powers of darkness and were tested in every way but did not sin. Send your angels to strengthen me in times of trial and help me imitate your fidelity to the Father's will.

Then the demons came out of the man and entered the swine, and the herd rushed down the steep bank into the lake and was drowned. Luke 8:33

Dealing With Deadly Demons

LUKE 8:26–39 *²⁶Then they arrived at the country of the Gerasenes, which is opposite Galilee. ²⁷As [Jesus] stepped out on land, a man of the city who had demons met him. For a long time he had worn no clothes, and he did not live in a house but in the tombs. ²⁸When he saw Jesus, he fell down before him and shouted at the top of his voice, "What have you to do with me, Jesus, Son of the Most High God? I beg you, do not torment me"— ²⁹for Jesus had commanded the unclean spirit to come out of the man. (For many times it had seized him; he was kept under guard and bound with chains and shackles, but he would break the bonds and be driven by the demon into the wilds.) ³⁰Jesus then asked him, "What is your name?" He said, "Legion"; for many demons had entered him. ³¹They begged him not to order them to go back into the abyss.*

³²Now there on the hillside a large herd of swine was feeding; and the demons begged Jesus to let them enter these. So he gave them permission. ³³Then the demons came out of the man and entered the swine, and the herd rushed down the steep bank into the lake and was drowned.

³⁴When the swineherds saw what had happened, they ran off and told it in the city and in the country. ³⁵Then people came out to see what had happened, and when they came to Jesus, they found the man from whom the demons had gone sitting at the feet of Jesus, clothed and in his right mind. And they were afraid.

³⁶ *Those who had seen it told them how the one who had been possessed by demons had been healed.* ³⁷ *Then all the people of the surrounding country of the Gerasenes asked Jesus to leave them; for they were seized with great fear. So he got into the boat and returned.* ³⁸ *The man from whom the demons had gone begged that he might be with him; but Jesus sent him away, saying,* ³⁹ *"Return to your home, and declare how much God has done for you." So he went away, proclaiming throughout the city how much Jesus had done for him.*

The concept that malevolent spirits or demons influenced people's lives and that certain formulas or rituals warded off their effects was held almost universally by people in the ancient world. Jewish literature at the time of Jesus elaborated on the origins and activities of demons, depicting them as fallen angels who had joined Satan in his revolt against God and able to enter the human personality causing sickness and distress. The gospel accounts take for granted the existence of these demons and attribute to them various kinds of afflictions, including violently insane behavior, the inability to speak, hear, or see, characteristics of epilepsy, and an inclination toward self-destruction.

The gospels describe the casting out of demons as a significant aspect of the ministry of Jesus, and also an important part of the authority Jesus conveyed to his disciples. Jesus' practice of expelling demons was in sharp contrast to the magical approach of other exorcists of the time, who used detailed incantations. The gospels demonstrate that Jesus cast out demons with his messianic authority, and rather than endowing his followers with specific techniques, they are simply endowed with his authority over the spirits.

The setting of this account and its grotesque outcome create an eerie mood. The demonized man was unclothed and lived in the tombs of the area. This miserable person had to be kept under guard, but often he would break the chains and shackles that bound him and be driven by his hostile spirits into the wilderness. When he saw Jesus he fell at his feet and shouted in the voice of the demons, "What have you to do with me, Jesus, Son of the Most High God?" (verses 27–29). Though apparently the man had never seen Jesus, the demons knew that he is God's agent, whose power far exceeds their own.

When Jesus asked the evil spirit his name, the spirit replied, "Legion" (verse 30). This is a Roman military term which suggests that Jesus faced a whole army of demons, whose collective power would be fierce. But realizing the greater power of Jesus, the demons begged him not to order them to go back into the "abyss" (verse 31). Jewish literature had described the abyss as the bottomless void into which Satan and all his demons would be cast at the final judgment. Instead Jesus sent them into a nearby heard of swine, which then stampeded down a steep bank and were drowned in the Sea of Galilee. Since the depth of the sea was often a symbol of the eternal abyss, this bizarre ending foreshadows the final reckoning when Satan's kingdom will be routed to the place of doom (see Jude 6).

The narrative makes clear that Jesus is in a non-Jewish area of Palestine. Everything about it is unclean and non-kosher—the tombs, the keepers of swine, and the alien territory—all suggesting a Gentile setting where observant Jews would not be found. Yet here the authority and healing power of Jesus is just as great as in Jewish Galilee, making it clear that there is no human disorder anywhere that Jesus cannot heal. The sight of the man from whom the demons had been cast "sitting at the feet of Jesus, clothed and in his right mind" (verse 35) is a sign for all to see that Jesus brings order, integration, and peace to tormented individuals and to a chaotic world.

Reflection and discussion

• What do the exorcisms performed by Jesus tell me about his power and authority? In what way do they enable me to trust in him?

• Psychology tells us that the causes of emotional disorders are multiple and complex. What are the demons that inflict struggling people today?

• What was the response of the people of the region to the work of Jesus (verses 35–37)? Why did they want Jesus to leave them?

• How do I imagine the man felt after his encounter with Jesus?

• What type of witness did Jesus assign to the man from whom he had cast the demons (verse 39)? How can I proclaim the good news of Jesus in this way?

Prayer

Jesus, Son of the Most High God, your power over evil is without limit or boundaries. Help me to trust in your authority over all evil spirits, and enable me to be a minister of your healing presence to those imprisoned in darkness and fear.

"When a strong man, fully armed, guards his castle, his property is safe. But when one stronger than he attacks him and overpowers him, he takes away his armor in which he trusted and divides his plunder. Luke 11:21–22

Satan's Kingdom Is Plundered

LUKE 10:17–20 ¹⁷*The seventy returned with joy, saying, "Lord, in your name even the demons submit to us!"* ¹⁸*He said to them, "I watched Satan fall from heaven like a flash of lightning.* ¹⁹*See, I have given you authority to tread on snakes and scorpions, and over all the power of the enemy; and nothing will hurt you.* ²⁰*Nevertheless, do not rejoice at this, that the spirits submit to you, but rejoice that your names are written in heaven."*

LUKE 11:14–26 ¹⁴*Now he was casting out a demon that was mute; when the demon had gone out, the one who had been mute spoke, and the crowds were amazed.* ¹⁵*But some of them said, "He casts out demons by Beelzebul, the ruler of the demons."* ¹⁶*Others, to test him, kept demanding from him a sign from heaven.* ¹⁷*But he knew what they were thinking and said to them, "Every kingdom divided against itself becomes a desert, and house falls on house.* ¹⁸*If Satan also is divided against himself, how will his kingdom stand? —for you say that I cast out the demons by Beelzebul.* ¹⁹*Now if I cast out the demons by Beelzebul, by whom do your exorcists cast them out? Therefore they will be your judges.* ²⁰*But if it is by the finger of God that I cast out the demons, then the kingdom of God has come to you.* ²¹*When a strong man, fully armed, guards his castle, his prop-*

erty is safe. ²²But when one stronger than he attacks him and overpowers him, he takes away his armor in which he trusted and divides his plunder. ²³Whoever is not with me is against me, and whoever does not gather with me scatters.

²⁴"When the unclean spirit has gone out of a person, it wanders through waterless regions looking for a resting place, but not finding any, it says, 'I will return to my house from which I came.' ²⁵When it comes, it finds it swept and put in order. ²⁶Then it goes and brings seven other spirits more evil than itself, and they enter and live there; and the last state of that person is worse than the first."

From a supernatural perspective, the ministry of Jesus is a battle with the forces of evil. The kingdom of God is in a fierce struggle with Satan and his minions. Jesus, who had demonstrated his power over demonic forces, has sent out seventy of his disciples with a share in his authority. Returning from battle, the seventy rejoice in their victory: "Lord, in your name even the demons submit to us!" (10:17). Jesus has given them power over the enemy, "authority to tread on snakes and scorpions" (10:19). These creatures that strike and sting their victims were sources of physical evil in ancient times and biblical symbols of all kinds of evil. God's words to the serpent in Genesis, "he will strike your head and you will strike his heal" (Gen 3:15), was often understood as a prophecy of the battle between the offspring of Eve and Satan. The crushing of the snake under the feet of Christ's disciples symbolizes God's power to destroy the prince of the demons: "The God of peace will shortly crush Satan under your feet" (Rom 16:20).

The battle of Christ and his disciples over evil will continue throughout the history of the church until the final judgment. Jesus' revelatory vision of Satan's defeat, "I watched Satan fall from heaven like a flash of lightning" (10:18), indicates that Christ's coming was the conquest of the devil, yet the implementation of that victory will be gradual, and still awaits its climactic conclusion. So Christ warns his disciples against a triumphal spirit. Our great joy should be, not that we have been given certain powers over evil, but that we share in the reign of God and are thus assured of the final victory (10:20).

The devil or Satan goes by a number of different names in the New Testament: Beelzebul, the ruler of the demons (11:15), the tempter, ruler of this world, god of this world, ruler of the power of the air, the evil one, the enemy, Beliar, the great dragon, and the ancient serpent. Under many guises the devil is the epitome of evil, always working at cross-purposes with God and humanity.

That Jesus would be accused of being in league with Beelzebul seems absurd. But the opponents of Jesus are blind to the signs of God's kingdom before them. The conflict is between two very real kingdoms, that of Satan and that of God. When Jesus or his delegates cast out demons, it is a sure sign that the kingdom of God has come among us (11:20). In Jesus' miniature parable, Satan is the strong man, heavily armed and standing guard over his castle. But a stronger ruler than Satan is making war on him and establishing his dominion on earth. Christ, the stronger one, is conquering the devil, stripping him of his armor, and claiming his possessions as booty (11:21–22). So we must choose sides; discipleship calls for decision. Choose the side of Christ and his kingdom, because his saving work is the beginning of the end for the forces of evil (11:23).

Removing the spirit of evil from our lives must always be accompanied by filling our lives with good. If not, more evil will return and our situation may become even worse. An empty life, like an empty house, invites intruders (11:24–26). When we fill our house with the riches of God's kingdom, swearing allegiance to the new sovereign, we can be assured that our dwelling will be protected against the intrusion of the evil one and his cronies.

Reflection and discussion

• In what ways is Christian discipleship like a battle? How do I equip myself for battle?

• Why does the ancient ritual of baptism include a bold statement to renounce Satan and all his works and all his empty promises?

• Why is a life that is spiritually neglected subject to the intrusion of evil spirits? What can I do to protect myself from the influences of the devil?

• What concerns and fears do I have about Satan and demons? What verse is most encouraging or comforting to me?

Prayer

Christ Jesus, you cast out the dark powers of Satan and welcome us into God's kingdom of light. Give me confidence in your authority over evil and help me to trust that you are Lord of heaven and earth.

For our struggle is not against enemies of blood and flesh, but against the rulers, against the authorities, against the cosmic powers of this present darkness, against the spiritual forces of evil in the heavenly places. Eph 6:12

Warfare Against a Deceptive Enemy

2 CORINTHIANS 11:13–15 *¹³For such boasters are false apostles, deceitful workers, disguising themselves as apostles of Christ. ¹⁴And no wonder! Even Satan disguises himself as an angel of light. ¹⁵So it is not strange if his ministers also disguise themselves as ministers of righteousness. Their end will match their deeds.*

EPHESIANS 6:10–18 *¹⁰Finally, be strong in the Lord and in the strength of his power. ¹¹Put on the whole armor of God, so that you may be able to stand against the wiles of the devil. ¹²For our struggle is not against enemies of blood and flesh, but against the rulers, against the authorities, against the cosmic powers of this present darkness, against the spiritual forces of evil in the heavenly places. ¹³Therefore take up the whole armor of God, so that you may be able to withstand on that evil day, and having done everything, to stand firm. ¹⁴Stand therefore, and fasten the belt of truth around your waist, and put on the breastplate of righteousness. ¹⁵As shoes for your feet put on whatever will make you ready to proclaim the gospel of peace. ¹⁶With all of these, take the shield of faith, with which you will be able to quench all the flaming arrows of the evil one. ¹⁷Take the helmet of salvation, and the sword of the Spirit, which is the word of God.*

¹⁸Pray in the Spirit at all times in every prayer and supplication. To that end keep alert and always persevere in supplication for all the saints.

The work of Satan is always deceptively attractive. We are never tempted by offers that are repulsive, that offer us personal or social ruin. The satanic temptation in the garden of Eden was the assurance, "you will be like God" (Gen 3:5), not "you will be like the devil." Jewish legend says that Satan disguised himself to seduce Eve to sin, and that he was successful by charming her rather than by terrifying her. In the wilderness Jesus was tempted to do things that were enticingly good: turning stones to loaves of bread (the hungry would certainly gain), leaping from the temple heights (those searching for proof of God's power would profit), take political control (the oppressed would benefit). The devil even quotes Scripture to make his tests seem more enticing.

In his second letter to the Corinthians Paul characterizes his opponents as "false apostles" who win over the people by disguising themselves as apostles of Christ. Paul compares this masquerading of his opponents with the work of Satan: "Even Satan disguises himself as an angel of light" (2 Cor 11:13–15). The prince of darkness covers up his true nature in order to attract his victims with illusionary promises. If Satan really had the cartoonish red suit complete with horns and pitchfork, he would be easy to identify. But his many disguises are alluring and his promises enthralling. Satan is indeed at war with humanity and one stratagem of war is to wear the enemy's uniform. In that way his armies can be penetrated and destroyed from within. Satan's warfare uses guerrilla tactics and deceptive strategy. Be ready for a different type of war.

In his letter to the Ephesians, Paul exhorts the Christian warrior to "put on the whole armor of God, so that you may be able to stand against the wiles of the devil" (Eph 6:11, 13). This concluding section of his letter reads like the speeches of generals in their "call to battle." It urges the army to be strong, determined, and alert. It points out the strengths of the enemy, but it urges the troops to stand firm, impressing upon them their own superior power and resources.

The enemies are spiritual, demonic forces: the devil, rulers, authorities, "the cosmic powers of this present darkness" (Eph 6:12). Likewise, the armor Christians have to face the dark powers are spiritual resources. Using the model of the Roman soldier preparing for battle, the believer must put on the belt of truth, the breastplate of righteousness, and the footwear of readiness to proclaim the gospel. The besieged believer must then take the shield of faith, the helmet of salvation, and the sword of God's word (Eph 6:14–17). The only real defense against these spiritual forces of evil is God's armor of ethical and spiritual virtues.

Finally, the ability to utilize all of God's armor calls for perseverance in prayer (Eph 6:18). A Christian must be watchful and constantly praying in the Spirit so as not to be caught off guard. Because all believers are involved in the spiritual battle and fighting alongside one another, prayer and supplication must transcend individualism and encompass all the saints.

Reflection and discussion

• What is the meaning and implication of Paul's saying, "Even Satan disguises himself as an angel of light" (2 Cor 11:14)?

• Which piece of God's armor do I need to "put on" to defend myself in my area of weakness, and what do I need to do to get that piece of armor ready for battle?

Prayer

Lord Jesus, you have led us in battle against the dark forces of our world and have given us the spiritual equipment we need to stand firm. Keep me constant and watchful in prayer so that I will not be caught off guard by the forces of the devil.

Discipline yourselves, keep alert. Like a roaring lion your adversary the devil prowls around, looking for someone to devour. 1 Pet 5:8

Vigilance and Resistance in the Face of the Adversary

1 PETER 5:6–11 *⁶Humble yourselves therefore under the mighty hand of God, so that he may exalt you in due time. ⁷Cast all your anxiety on him, because he cares for you. ⁸Discipline yourselves, keep alert. Like a roaring lion your adversary the devil prowls around, looking for someone to devour. ⁹Resist him, steadfast in your faith, for you know that your brothers and sisters in all the world are undergoing the same kinds of suffering. ¹⁰And after you have suffered for a little while, the God of all grace, who has called you to his eternal glory in Christ, will himself restore, support, strengthen, and establish you. ¹¹To him be the power forever and ever. Amen.*

In the closing words of his first letter, Peter urges humility and serenity in the face of God (verses 6–7), and vigilance and resistance in the face of the devil (verses 8–9). He assures suffering Christians that their distress is only for a time, that God's ultimate goal for his people is "eternal glory in Christ" (verse 10).

To be humble means that we understand the truth about the reality of God and our relationship to him. It means recognizing that "the mighty hand of God" is the source of all that we are and that we are absolutely dependent on him. God's mighty hand remains in control of events in our lives and gives us confidence in his protection and guidance. With humble trust we can be confident about the future because we know that he will exalt us at the right time (verse 6). So we can let go of all our anxiety and leave it with God. No matter how trying life is at times, we can let God handle our worry because he is personally concerned for each of us. Not only is God an all-powerful deity who is able to deliver us from our fears, but he is a God who is willing and wanting to deliver us (verse 7).

Though we can be humble and serene before God, we must be vigilant and resistant before the devil. This expresses the healthy respect for the power of evil that we find throughout the New Testament. The manifestation of evil in the world is not confined to the understandable world of individual human choice. The world is battered by the power of transcendent forces of evil which holds humanity in its grip. The biblical respect for evil is served neither by an exaggerated obsession with demons nor by modern skepticism of evil forces. Recognizing the cosmic dimensions of evil does not lessen the human responsibility to work toward the elimination of social injustices and human suffering, but rather compels us to ally our efforts with the God who has ultimately defeated evil and will vanquish it in due time.

The devil prowls around like a roaring lion, looking for someone to devour (verse 8). Sometimes a lion paralyzes its prey with its terrifying roar; at other times it stalks its victims silently. The prince of evil is like the king of the jungle; both are masters in the hunting arts. The Christian therefore must be disciplined and alert, aware that the foe may attack anywhere at any time.

In the face of the powers of evil, Peter urges Christians to "resist him, steadfast in your faith" (verse 9). In standing up to the devil's powers, we can neither underestimate him nor rely only on our own strength. Alone we are no match for his might and prowess, so we must stand firm in our faith. We are united with brothers and sisters throughout the world who are caught up in the same struggles. Though persecution and suffering are different from place to place around the world, just as it was in the first century when Peter wrote, the world itself is in many respects a hostile environment for those called to eternal glory in Christ.

Though suffering often seems interminable, it is really only "for a little while" (verse 10). It will not go on forever; it will come to an end. And though suffering often seems meaningless, it does have a purpose, as Peter stresses throughout his letter. God uses our every experience, perhaps especially the most difficult ones, to further his loving purpose in the lives of his people. Peter mentions four results of suffering endured in faith: it serves to "restore" the weaknesses in our character, to "support" or make solid our character, to "strengthen" our trust, and to "establish" a foundation that cannot be shaken. Our suffering is redemptive and part of Christ's cosmic transformation in which the power of evil will be overcome and the world will find its way to God.

Our God is "the God of all grace." Beyond the present anxiety and trials lies the glory to come in the future. The difficult experiences of this life are limited. What lies ahead for us in the purposes of God is eternal. Faith in this God who supports and strengthens us is a great consolation when the days are dark and threatening. Challenged and comforted by such a God, we can only respond: "To him be the power for ever and ever. Amen."

Reflection and discussion

• Why is the lion an effective image for the work of the devil? How can I, like Daniel, be delivered from the mouth of the lion?

• How can genuine humility give me greater confidence and freedom from anxiety?

Prayer

God of all grace, you have called me to a future of eternal glory in Christ. Assure me of your care so that I can freely cast all my anxieties on you. Keep me steadfast in faith and united with my suffering brothers and sisters throughout the world.

The great dragon was thrown down, that ancient serpent, who is called the Devil and Satan, the deceiver of the whole world—he was thrown down to the earth, and his angels were thrown down with him. Rev 12:9

Michael Defeats the World's Deceiver

REVELATION 12:7–12 *⁷And war broke out in heaven; Michael and his angels fought against the dragon. The dragon and his angels fought back, ⁸but they were defeated, and there was no longer any place for them in heaven. ⁹The great dragon was thrown down, that ancient serpent, who is called the Devil and Satan, the deceiver of the whole world—he was thrown down to the earth, and his angels were thrown down with him.*

¹⁰Then I heard a loud voice in heaven, proclaiming,

"Now have come the salvation and the power
  and the kingdom of our God
  and the authority of his Messiah,
for the accuser of our comrades has been thrown down,
  who accuses them day and night before our God.
¹¹But they have conquered him by the blood of the Lamb
  and by the word of their testimony,
for they did not cling to life even in the face of death.
¹²Rejoice then, you heavens
  and those who dwell in them!
But woe to the earth and the sea,

for the devil has come down to you
with great wrath,
because he knows that his time is short!"

The very real struggle between God's saving will and the forces of evil is given vivid pictorial dramatization in the book of Revelation. The battle in heaven is fought between Michael and his angels and the dragon and his angels. The defeat of the dragon expresses on a cosmic plane the transcendent effects of the life, death, and resurrection of Christ.

Michael the archangel is first mentioned by name in the book of Daniel. He is God's great prince, the protector of God's people (Dan 10:13, 21; 12:1), the patron angel of Israel. In extra-biblical Jewish literature he is the captain of the angelic hosts and the leader of the archangels. The dragon represents the vastness of the reservoir of evil by which the world is threatened and from which we cannot deliver ourselves. By identifying the dragon with Satan, the devil, and the ancient serpent (verse 9), the author intends to symbolize all the forces of evil that seek to ensnare humanity, beginning in the garden of Eden and continuing throughout the biblical narratives.

The most prominent Old Testament description of the role of Satan appears in the prologue of the book of Job. The "Satan" (adversary, accuser) appears with the divine council. It is uncertain whether he is a legitimate member of the heavenly assembly or whether he is an intruder. This uncertainty is evoked by God's question to him, "Where have you come from?" (Job 1:7; 2:2). Like a lawyer for the other side, he holds the task of indicting and prosecuting sinners before the bar of divine justice. He wanders to and fro on the earth observing humans, reporting back on the state of their loyalty to God, and trying to coax people into committing sins for which they can then be punished (Job 1:6–12; 2:1–7; 1 Chron 21:1). Later Jewish literature identified Satan with the serpent in Eden and with the evil inclination which infects humanity.

As proclaimed in the heavenly song that interprets the action, the expulsion of Satan from heaven is the result of the victory of Christ on earth (verses 10–12). It is similar to the vision of Jesus reported in Luke 10:18, "I watched Satan fall from heaven like a flash of lightening." Christians are not just passive beneficiaries; they too are involved in Satan's defeat. The blood of their martyrdom flows together with the blood of the Lamb. Their "testimony" is that "they did not cling to life even in the face of death" (verse 11).

Satan is described as "the accuser," the one who accused the people of the earth in the heavenly court, trying to find them guilty and deserving of punishment (verse 10). Christians are acquitted in that court because of Christ's death and resurrection, accompanied by the faithful "testimony" of his followers. God is no longer willing to listen to Satan's accusations of God's people, for they have been forgiven. The counterpart of "the accuser" is the Spirit of truth, "the Advocate," who prosecutes the world and its evil ruler and proves them wrong about sin, righteousness, and judgment (John 16:7–8). The new age of divine victory over evil, the kingdom of God, has begun.

Though the devil and his angels are already defeated in the transcendent world, they have been cast down to this world, frustrated and angry. This explains why the church's struggle has not ended. The battle continues on earth, but the power of Satan has been broken. His influence is limited and his days are numbered (verse 12).

Reflection and discussion

• How does the life, death, and resurrection of Christ change the role of Satan?

• How is the power and influence of Satan overcome (verse 11)? How can I apply this strategy to my own life?

Prayer

Lamb of God, who takes away the sins of the world, have mercy on us. With your blood you have conquered the powers of Satan and his cynical accusations. Protect us against his great wrath and grant us peace.

SUGGESTIONS FOR FACILITATORS, GROUP SESSION 5

1. Welcome group members and ask if anyone has any questions, announcements, or requests.

2. You may want to pray this prayer as a group:

Lord God, you allowed your Son to be tempted by the devil, but he chose your saving will even in his greatest weakness and pain. You have given each of us a free will and the ability to willingly choose you over the superficial and temporary attractions of the world. Give us the desire and the courage to always choose your will and your kingdom over the powers of darkness and evil. Send Michael and his minions to defend us in battle and give us the confidence that Satan and his legions have been ultimately defeated. And when our life is over, welcome us into the glories of your eternal kingdom, where you live and reign forever.

3. Ask one or more of the following questions:
   - What most intrigued you from this week's study?
   - How can awareness of the work of Satan help you in your relationship with Jesus?

4. Discuss lessons 19 through 24. Choose one or more of the questions for reflection and discussion from each lesson to talk over as a group.

5. Ask the group members to name one thing they have most appreciated about the way the group has worked during this Bible study. Ask group members to discuss any changes they might suggest in the way the group works in future studies.

6. Invite group members to complete lessons 25 through 30 on their own during the six days before the next meeting. They should write out their own answers to the questions as preparation for next week's session.

7. Discuss how angels and demons have influenced art, film, media, and modern culture.

8. Conclude by praying aloud together the prayer at the end of one of the lessons discussed. You may want to conclude the prayer by asking members to voice prayers of thanksgiving.

David looked up and saw the angel of the Lord standing between earth and
heaven, and in his hand a drawn sword stretched out over Jerusalem.

1 Chron 21:16

The Angel Puts His Sword
Back into its Sheath

1 CHRONICLES 21:8—22:1 ⁸*David said to God, "I have sinned greatly
in that I have done this thing. But now, I pray you, take away the guilt of your
servant; for I have done very foolishly."* ⁹*The Lord spoke to Gad, David's seer, saying,* ¹⁰*"Go and say to David, 'Thus says the Lord: Three things I offer you; choose
one of them, so that I may do it to you.'"* ¹¹*So Gad came to David and said to
him, "Thus says the Lord, 'Take your choice:* ¹²*either three years of famine; or
three months of devastation by your foes, while the sword of your enemies over-
takes you; or three days of the sword of the Lord, pestilence on the land, and the
angel of the Lord destroying throughout all the territory of Israel.' Now decide
what answer I shall return to the one who sent me."* ¹³*Then David said to Gad,
"I am in great distress; let me fall into the hand of the Lord, for his mercy is very
great; but let me not fall into human hands."*

¹⁴*So the Lord sent a pestilence on Israel; and seventy thousand persons fell in
Israel.* ¹⁵*And God sent an angel to Jerusalem to destroy it; but when he was about
to destroy it, the Lord took note and relented concerning the calamity; he said to
the destroying angel, "Enough! Stay your hand." The angel of the Lord was then
standing by the threshing floor of Ornan the Jebusite.* ¹⁶*David looked up and saw
the angel of the Lord standing between earth and heaven, and in his hand a*

drawn sword stretched out over Jerusalem. Then David and the elders, clothed in sackcloth, fell on their faces. [17]And David said to God, "Was it not I who gave the command to count the people? It is I who have sinned and done very wickedly. But these sheep, what have they done? Let your hand, I pray, O Lord my God, be against me and against my father's house; but do not let your people be plagued!"

[18]Then the angel of the Lord commanded Gad to tell David that he should go up and erect an altar to the Lord on the threshing floor of Ornan the Jebusite. [19]So David went up following Gad's instructions, which he had spoken in the name of the Lord. [20]Ornan turned and saw the angel; and while his four sons who were with him hid themselves, Ornan continued to thresh wheat. [21]As David came to Ornan, Ornan looked and saw David; he went out from the threshing floor, and did obeisance to David with his face to the ground. [22]David said to Ornan, "Give me the site of the threshing floor that I may build on it an altar to the Lord—give it to me at its full price—so that the plague may be averted from the people." [23]Then Ornan said to David, "Take it; and let my lord the king do what seems good to him; see, I present the oxen for burnt offerings, and the threshing sledges for the wood, and the wheat for a grain offering. I give it all." [24]But King David said to Ornan, "No; I will buy them for the full price. I will not take for the Lord what is yours, nor offer burnt offerings that cost me nothing." [25]So David paid Ornan six hundred shekels of gold by weight for the site. [26]David built there an altar to the Lord and presented burnt offerings and offerings of well-being. He called upon the Lord, and he answered him with fire from heaven on the altar of burnt offering. [27]Then the Lord commanded the angel, and he put his sword back into its sheath.

[28]At that time, when David saw that the Lord had answered him at the threshing floor of Ornan the Jebusite, he made his sacrifices there. [29]For the tabernacle of the Lord, which Moses had made in the wilderness, and the altar of burnt offering were at that time in the high place at Gibeon; [30]but David could not go before it to inquire of God, for he was afraid of the sword of the angel of the Lord.

22

[1]Then David said, "Here shall be the house of the Lord God and here the altar of burnt offering for Israel."

In addition to the multiple roles of angels in the Bible as messengers, mediators, guardians, rescuers, and guides, the angels are also ministers of God's judgment. The angel of God, standing between heaven and earth, with a sword in his hand stretched out over Jerusalem, was sent to execute the just consequences of King David's grave sin. As we know from our own sinfulness, even when we recognize our sin and repent, we still experience the consequences of our sinful deeds. The distinction between the destroying angel and the actions of God express the differences between the justice that our sins demand and the merciful will of God toward us (verse 15).

We are not told the exact nature of David's great sin as king of Israel. It is somehow related to taking a counting of the people of Israel (verse 17). While there is nothing wrong with taking a census, the action was probably associated with David's pride in his own achievements and overconfidence in the military might of his nation. Realizing the dreadfulness of his action, David repented and asked for forgiveness (verse 8). God's answer came through David's prophet, Gad. David is given a terrible choice: three years of famine, three months of war, or three days of plague (verses 9–12). The shorter the time the more serious the effects, but each option would lead to national devastation, lessening the numbers of which David had been so proud.

In ordering the census, David was a typical imperial leader; in his response to God, he is an exemplary man of faith. His choice of punishment is an expression of his trust in God: "Let me fall into the hand of the Lord, for his mercy is very great, but let me not fall into human hands" (verse 13). Three days of plague was the choice that seemed at the time to be the most direct "act of God." Famine would have made his nation dependent on grain merchants; war would have put his people at the mercy of their enemies. David believed that God's punishment would be no more than they deserved for the satisfaction of justice, and that there would be mercy only from God, certainly not from anyone else.

When the pestilence sweeps through the land, seventy thousand people die as a result. But then, with the destroying angel poised over Jerusalem itself, God said to the angel, "Enough! Stay your hand" (verse 14–15). When David saw the awful vision of the angel with the drawn sword, he cried out for God to hold him alone responsible and to spare the people of Jerusalem (verses 16–17). In response, God's angel instructed David through his prophet Gad to erect an altar on the site (verse 18).

The angel had appeared on the mount north of Jerusalem. It was the site used by Ornan the Jebusite for threshing grain. Ornan and his sons also see the angel; however, while his four sons hide from the vision, Ornan goes on threshing grain (verse 20). Yet when David came to Ornan to acquire the site of his threshing floor, Ornan bowed profoundly to his king. When David declared why he wanted the site, Ornan spontaneously offered him not only the site, but his oxen and grain for the sacrifice and threshing-sledges for the firewood. David, however, insisted on paying the full price, and he purchased the high place for six hundred shekels of gold (verses 21–25).

When David built the altar and placed the offerings upon it, God demonstrated his acceptance of David's sacrifice by sending fire from heaven upon the altar (verse 26). Then, in a simple but powerful expression of God's mercy, the narrative states: "Then the Lord commanded the angel, and he put his sword back into its sheath." (verse 27). This place where God demonstrated his sovereign mercy to his king and his people became the place where David's son Solomon would build the great temple for the worship of God.

Reflection and discussion

• Why did David experience punishment even after he had repented of his grave sin? Why does the punishment fall on Israel and not just David?

• Why did David choose the third choice for his punishment? How was his choice an expression of his trust in God?

• Did David's sacrifice cause God to relent in mercy, or did God first relent and David offered the sacrifice in response to God's mercy? What does the ambiguity indicate about God's grace and our expressions of trust?

• What does this account teach me about the relationship between God's justice and God's mercy?

• What is the significance of this place being chosen as the site of Jerusalem's future temple?

Prayer

God of justice and mercy, you are merciful toward those who trust in you. Forgive me for my sins and do not punish me as my sins deserve. As I offer my prayers and sufferings to you, fill me with the peace of knowing you and experiencing your grace.

"The harvest is the end of the age, and the reapers are angels." Matt 13:39

The Final Separation of the Weeds from the Wheat

MATTHEW 13:24–30, 36–43 [24] *[Jesus] put before them another parable: "The kingdom of heaven may be compared to someone who sowed good seed in his field; [25] but while everybody was asleep, an enemy came and sowed weeds among the wheat, and then went away. [26] So when the plants came up and bore grain, then the weeds appeared as well. [27] And the slaves of the householder came and said to him, 'Master, did you not sow good seed in your field? Where, then, did these weeds come from?' [28] He answered, 'An enemy has done this.' The slaves said to him, 'Then do you want us to go and gather them?' [29] But he replied, 'No; for in gathering the weeds you would uproot the wheat along with them. [30] Let both of them grow together until the harvest; and at harvest time I will tell the reapers, Collect the weeds first and bind them in bundles to be burned, but gather the wheat into my barn.'"*

[36] *Then he left the crowds and went into the house. And his disciples approached him, saying, "Explain to us the parable of the weeds of the field." [37] He answered, "The one who sows the good seed is the Son of Man; [38] the field is the world, and the good seed are the children of the kingdom; the weeds are the children of the evil one, [39] and the enemy who sowed them is the devil; the harvest is the end of the age, and the reapers are angels. [40] Just as the weeds are collected and burned up with fire, so will it be at the end of the age. [41] The Son of Man will send his angels, and they will collect out of his kingdom all causes of*

111

sin and all evildoers, ⁴²*and they will throw them into the furnace of fire, where there will be weeping and gnashing of teeth.* ⁴³*Then the righteous will shine like the sun in the kingdom of their Father. Let anyone with ears listen!"*

The parables of Jesus explain that the angels are indeed ministers of God's justice, but not until the last judgment at the end of time. Jesus' parable of the wheat and the weeds creates a contrast between God's kingdom as it exists now in its imperfect form on earth and the final fullness of the kingdom to come. The work of Christ and the work of the devil intermingle in the world until the final days when Christ will send his angels to remove all causes of sin and all evildoers in order to present the final and perfect kingdom to the Father.

In the parable Jesus said the kingdom is like the situation of a householder who sowed good seed in his field, but an enemy came at night and sowed weeds among the wheat. The type of weed he mentions looks at first very much like the growing wheat. But by the time the grain appears and the difference becomes obvious, the roots of the weeds are so entwined with those of the wheat that uprooting the one might endanger the other. The householder wisely tells his slaves to let them grow together until harvest time. Only then will the reapers collect the weeds and tie them in bundles to be used for fuel and gather the grain into the barn.

The application to the life of the church is clear enough, even without Jesus' allegorical interpretation. In the present age, there will always be a mixture of good and evil, saints and sinners. Jesus uses these images to convey that human beings are not capable of making the kinds of judgments implied in separating the weeds from the wheat. In pulling out what they think are weeds, they may very well be pulling up wheat. Only God can make these kinds of judgments, and at the proper time he will. The church should not take the role of God and try to purify itself with purges and expulsions. With proper patience, it may even be possible for weeds to become wheat.

In the allegorical interpretation that follows the parable, Jesus offers a list of seven equivalencies to decode the parable (verses 37–39). The sower of the good seed is the risen Christ and the good seed are the children of God's kingdom. The enemy who sowed the weeds is the devil and the weeds are the children of the evil one. The field is the world, which is the present setting for the kingdom. The time of harvest is a frequent biblical image for the last judgment, which is here called "the end of the age," signifying both the conclusion and the fulfillment of this world and its history. The angels are the agents of God's judgment who will pluck out the "evildoers" from the kingdom so that the "righteous" will shine in God's eternal reign (verses 41–43).

Reflection and discussion

• Why are human beings incapable of separating the weeds from the wheat? Why is this task left to the angels at the end of time?

• In what way can strident and overzealous judgment of the world's evils harm our mission as disciples of Jesus in the world? In what way does the teaching of Jesus encourage a spirit of patience, mercy, and tolerance in the church?

Prayer

Lord of the kingdom, you have sown the seeds of the gospel in our world and you await the good fruit of our service. Help me to water the ground, fertilize the field, and produce the yield of merciful love.

He will send out his angels with a loud trumpet call, and they will gather his elect from the four winds, from one end of heaven to the other. Matt 24:31

The Glorious Coming of Christ

MATTHEW 24:29–31

²⁹*"Immediately after the suffering of those days*
the sun will be darkened,
and the moon will not give its light;
the stars will fall from heaven,
and the powers of heaven will be shaken.
³⁰*Then the sign of the Son of Man will appear in heaven, and then all the tribes of the earth will mourn, and they will see 'the Son of Man coming on the clouds of heaven' with power and great glory.* ³¹*And he will send out his angels with a loud trumpet call, and they will gather his elect from the four winds, from one end of heaven to the other."*

MATTHEW 25:31–33 ³¹*"When the Son of Man comes in his glory, and all the angels with him, then he will sit on the throne of his glory.* ³²*All the nations will be gathered before him, and he will separate people one from another as a shepherd separates the sheep from the goats,* ³³*and he will put the sheep at his right hand and the goats at the left."*

Toward the end of the public ministry of Jesus, he taught about the coming fulfillment of all things. The purpose of these teachings was to give his followers hope and to urge them to be watchful. Since it is not ours to know the time of Christ's glorious appearing, we must live each day in the light of his coming. Though angels surround us—guarding and guiding us along life's path—they will have an exceptional role when they accompany Christ at the end of time to gather the faithful into God's eternal kingdom.

The coming of Christ in glory is presented in the New Testament as an event to be anticipated with joyful hope. He will come to end the suffering of the present world. The images of the cosmic disturbances marking the end of the world are taken from the prophets of the Old Testament. Similar language is used in the book of Revelation. The "sign of the Son of Man" that will appear in heaven is the glorified Christ himself (24:30). His will be a universal appearing that will be manifested to all people. The image of "the Son of Man coming on the clouds of heaven" is from the writings of the prophet Daniel. This human-like figure in Daniel was given "dominion and glory and kingship." His authority is an "everlasting dominion," never to be destroyed, and "all peoples, nations, and languages should serve him" (Dan 7:13–14). Jesus applied this text to himself, and early Christians found that Daniel's words expressed their conviction that the crucified Jesus would return as the glorified Christ.

The trumpet was used in ancient Israel to gather God's people for religious purposes, for the announcement of kings, and to signal activities on the battlefield. Here the trumpet call accompanies the glorious coming of Christ who sends out his angels to gather God's elect from all corners of the world (24:31). A similar image is offered by Paul: "The Lord himself, with a cry of command, with the archangel's call and with the sound of God's trumpet, will descend from heaven" (1 Thes 4:16–17). The call of God's archangel and the sound of the trumpet accompany the glorious coming of Christ. Then those who have died will rise and together with those still living will be raised into the clouds to welcome the coming of the triumphant Christ.

The final instruction of Jesus in Matthew's gospel presents the final judgment. Its primary purpose is to teach the criterion by which the Son of Man will judge the people of every nation. Those welcomed into the kingdom are those who recognize Christ in people who are hungry, thirsty, estranged, naked, sick, and imprisoned. To be watchful and ready for Christ's return means to be attentive to Christ in the needs of these least ones—the poor and outcast and oppressed. The glorious Son of Man is pictured with divine majesty: he comes in his glory, all the angels are with him, he sits on his glorious throne (25:31). The people of all the nations of the world are gathered around him, like a flock gathered by its shepherd (25:32).

Reflection and discussion

• Why is the glorious coming of Christ something I can anticipate with joyful hope rather than fearful gloom?

• If I knew that Christ would return at a specific time this year, what changes would I make in my life? What hinders me from making those changes right now?

Prayer

Glorious Son of Man, you will come again in glory to judge the living and the dead. Keep me watchful and ready for your future coming, but don't let me neglect to see your presence each day in the least of my brothers and sisters.

Bless the Lord, O you his angels, you mighty ones who do his bidding, obedient to his spoken word. Ps 103:20

Let All Creatures Praise the Lord

PSALM 89:5–8

⁵Let the heavens praise your wonders, O Lord,
  your faithfulness in the assembly of the holy ones.
⁶For who in the skies can be compared to the Lord?
  Who among the heavenly beings is like the Lord,
⁷a God feared in the council of the holy ones,
  great and awesome above all that are around him?
⁸O Lord God of hosts,
  who is as mighty as you, O Lord?
  Your faithfulness surrounds you.

PSALM 103:19–22

¹⁹The Lord has established his throne in the heavens,
  and his kingdom rules over all.
²⁰Bless the Lord, O you his angels,
  you mighty ones who do his bidding,
  obedient to his spoken word.
²¹Bless the Lord, all his hosts,
  his ministers that do his will.

²²*Bless the Lord, all his works,*
in all places of his dominion.
Bless the Lord, O my soul.

PSALM 148:1–5

¹*Praise the Lord!*
Praise the Lord from the heavens;
praise him in the heights!
²*Praise him, all his angels;*
praise him, all his host!
³*Praise him, sun and moon;*
praise him, all you shining stars!
⁴*Praise him, you highest heavens,*
and you waters above the heavens!
⁵*Let them praise the name of the Lord,*
for he commanded and they were created.

The faith of ancient Israel and of Christianity proclaims God as the Creator of heaven and earth. The scriptural expression "heaven and earth" means all that exists, creation in its entirety, "all that is seen and unseen." God made a spiritual, angelic order of creation, and he made an earthly, corporeal order. God's human creation, composed of both spirit and body, is a unique unity of both orders of creation.

Psalm 89 evokes the scene of the divine council assembled in heaven. There God reigns as the mighty God of the heavenly hosts, the universal king. He is surrounded by heavenly beings, "the assembly of the holy ones" (89:5, 7) who praise him continually. The quality of God praised above all is his incomparable "faithfulness" (89:5, 8). The enduring stability of the cosmos is a visible expression of God's consistency and constant concern for all his creatures. Because the throne of God is the source of all authority and the origin of God's fidelity expressed in the covenant, God's people can trust completely in his loving care.

Psalm 103 offers praise to God, beginning with the individual psalmist, then fanning out to the community of Israel, to the whole of humanity, and finally to all creation. The conclusion of the psalm calls on all the angels of God's heavenly court—mighty ones, God's ministers, and all his hosts—to join with all creation in blessing the Lord (103:20–21). Because God's throne is established in the heavens, his kingdom rules over all creation (103:19), the visible world on earth and the invisible creation in heaven. The word "all" occurs four times in the final four verses—God rules over all, all his hosts, all his works, in all places—reinforcing a sweeping sense of completeness and totality. The final soliloquy, "Bless the Lord, O my soul" (103:22), sets the context of our individual worship of God within the context of a universal chorus.

As the book of Psalms draws to its close, the call to praise God rises to its final crescendo. Psalm 148 is the third in the group of five Hallelujah psalms that conclude the book. All the psalms in this collection open and close with "Praise the Lord," and this psalm repeats the call throughout. All creation is invited to join in the praise of God, beginning with praise "from the heavens," from "all his angels, all his hosts" (148:1–2). These heavenly choirs join with the sun and moon and stars, and even the highest heavens and the cosmic waters above the heavens, to adore their Creator. As the psalm continues, it includes all the earth: creatures of the sea, weather, mountains, trees, animals, rulers, and all people of the world. The psalm recruits the entire realm of being to express its praise of God.

The highest and most perfect action of any creature is to praise its Creator. The Lord is praised as the supreme ruler who created all that exists by the authority of his commanding word and orders all creation according to his purpose (148:5). The entire universe is the sacred place for worshipping God. Angels, humans beings, animals, and all creatures, animate and inanimate, praise God in their very being and doing, by existing and fulfilling their assigned place. As God's people, we give praise with the angels in heaven to the Creator whose name alone is exalted and whose majesty is above heaven and earth.

Reflection and discussion

• If a tree praises God by fulfilling its created purpose as a tree, how do I best praise God? How do the angels best praise God?

• How do human beings share in both the earthly and heavenly orders of God's creation? In what way are we like the angels?

• When do I most experience contact with the invisible world of God's spiritual creation? How does contemplating God's heavenly reign help me to trust in God's fidelity?

• In what way do these psalms help me to experience the unity and holiness of all God's creation?

Prayer

Magnificent Lord, I praise your majesty together with all creation in heaven and on earth. All things visible and invisible give you glory. In the presence of the angels, I bless your holy name. Bless the Lord, O my soul.

Day and night without ceasing they sing, "Holy, holy, holy, the Lord God the Almighty, who was and is and is to come." Rev 4:8

Praise of God as Creator and Redeemer

REVELATION 4:1–11 *¹After this I looked, and there in heaven a door stood open! And the first voice, which I had heard speaking to me like a trumpet, said, "Come up here, and I will show you what must take place after this." ²At once I was in the spirit, and there in heaven stood a throne, with one seated on the throne! ³And the one seated there looks like jasper and carnelian, and around the throne is a rainbow that looks like an emerald. ⁴Around the throne are twenty-four thrones, and seated on the thrones are twenty-four elders, dressed in white robes, with golden crowns on their heads. ⁵Coming from the throne are flashes of lightning, and rumblings and peals of thunder, and in front of the throne burn seven flaming torches, which are the seven spirits of God; ⁶and in front of the throne there is something like a sea of glass, like crystal.*

Around the throne, and on each side of the throne, are four living creatures, full of eyes in front and behind: ⁷the first living creature like a lion, the second living creature like an ox, the third living creature with a face like a human face, and the fourth living creature like a flying eagle. ⁸And the four living creatures, each of them with six wings, are full of eyes all around and inside. Day and night without ceasing they sing,

"Holy, holy, holy,
the Lord God the Almighty,

who was and is and is to come."

⁹*And whenever the living creatures give glory and honor and thanks to the one who is seated on the throne, who lives forever and ever,* ¹⁰*the twenty-four elders fall before the one who is seated on the throne and worship the one who lives forever and ever; they cast their crowns before the throne, singing,*

¹¹*"You are worthy, our Lord and God,*
   to receive glory and honor and power,
for you created all things,
   and by your will they existed and were created."

REVELATION 5:1–8 ¹*Then I saw in the right hand of the one seated on the throne a scroll written on the inside and on the back, sealed with seven seals;* ²*and I saw a mighty angel proclaiming with a loud voice, "Who is worthy to open the scroll and break its seals?"* ³*And no one in heaven or on earth or under the earth was able to open the scroll or to look into it.* ⁴*And I began to weep bitterly because no one was found worthy to open the scroll or to look into it.* ⁵*Then one of the elders said to me, "Do not weep. See, the Lion of the tribe of Judah, the Root of David, has conquered, so that he can open the scroll and its seven seals."* ⁶*Then I saw between the throne and the four living creatures and among the elders a Lamb standing as if it had been slaughtered, having seven horns and seven eyes, which are the seven spirits of God sent out into all the earth.* ⁷*He went and took the scroll from the right hand of the one who was seated on the throne.* ⁸*When he had taken the scroll, the four living creatures and the twenty-four elders fell before the Lamb, each holding a harp and golden bowls full of incense, which are the prayers of the saints.*

An open door and the trumpet-like voice of an angel invite John, the prophetic seer and writer of Revelation, to enter into a vision of heaven. The angels that fill the book of Revelation have numerous roles: bearers of revelation, guides to the action, interpreters of the visions, and participants in the heavenly worship of God. The vision offers John and his readers a wondrous impression of divine majesty, evoking praise of God and a realization of God's sovereignty over all creation and events.

The heavenly vision is dominated by the throne, a symbol of God's sovereign splendor and authority. The divine throne room is also the heavenly control room, where God and the Lamb are worshipped and where permission is given for future events to unfold. It assures John and the readers that God's gracious purpose for the universe will come to pass. The one seated on the throne is described with the colorful and luminous splendor of jewels and the rainbow (4:2–3). The flashes of lightning and peals of thunder coming from the throne evoke the divine presence as experienced at Mount Sinai and other ancient manifestations of God on earth (4:5).

The "four living creatures" that surround the throne of God are angel-like beings described with the characteristics of the cherubim and seraphim in the visions of Ezekiel and Isaiah (Ezek 1:4–14; Isa 6:1–8). Each of these beings share the likeness of the highest, most noble creature of its species: the eagle is the most glorious among the birds, the ox the most noble among the domestic animals, the lion among the wild animals, and the human the highest of all (4:7). They represent the praise of all living creation. The hymn they sing echoes the Trishagion ("Thrice Holy") of the seraphim in Isaiah's vision in the temple. This superlatively holy God is the Lord of the ages, the one "who was and is and is to come" (4:8). This God is Lord over all life, spiritual and material, and is worthy to receive "glory and honor and power" (4:11).

Within the throne room John's eyes fasten on the sealed scroll in the hand of God, a symbol of God's plan for the conclusion of salvation's history. The mighty angel is unable to find one who is worthy or able to open its seven seals. Sadly for all, the unfolding salvation of the world is at a standstill (5:1–4). Then comes the announcement that only one is worthy and has earned the right to open the sealed scroll. This one is the Lion of Judah, an ancient title for the Davidic Messiah. Yet, when John expected a mighty Lion to appear, he saw a Lamb, slain though standing, in the midst of the heavenly assembly (5:5–6). The Lamb of God, the sacrificed and risen Christ, will open God's sealed plan and carry out the final victory over evil and death. He is the Lion and the Lamb, the King and Redeemer. From the perspective of heaven, he has already triumphed; from the viewpoint of earth, the final victory is still to come. All the heavenly court bows before the throne of the Lamb, and offers through music and incense the hopeful prayers of God's people (5:7–8).

Reflection and discussion

• What would this vision have meant for the persecuted Christians of the late first century? What does it mean for me?

• In what ways do the four living creatures share characteristics of the seraphim and cherubim in the visions of Isaiah and Ezekiel?

• How is Christ like both a Lion and a Lamb? Why is he alone worthy to open the scroll?

Prayer

Majestic God, you are worthy to receive glory and honor and power. Through Christ the angels of heaven offer their prayer of adoration as they rejoice in your presence forever. May our voices be one with theirs in their triumphant hymn of praise.

And I saw another mighty angel coming down from heaven, wrapped in a cloud, with a rainbow over his head; his face was like the sun, and his legs like pillars of fire. Rev 10:1

Awaiting the Glorious Kingdom of God

REVELATION 8:1–6 *¹When the Lamb opened the seventh seal, there was silence in heaven for about half an hour. ²And I saw the seven angels who stand before God, and seven trumpets were given to them. ³Another angel with a golden censer came and stood at the altar; he was given a great quantity of incense to offer with the prayers of all the saints on the golden altar that is before the throne. ⁴And the smoke of the incense, with the prayers of the saints, rose before God from the hand of the angel. ⁵Then the angel took the censer and filled it with fire from the altar and threw it on the earth; and there were peals of thunder, rumblings, flashes of lightning, and an earthquake. ⁶Now the seven angels who had the seven trumpets made ready to blow them.*

REVELATION 10:1–7 *¹And I saw another mighty angel coming down from heaven, wrapped in a cloud, with a rainbow over his head; his face was like the sun, and his legs like pillars of fire. ²He held a little scroll open in his hand. Setting his right foot on the sea and his left foot on the land, ³he gave a great shout, like a lion roaring. And when he shouted, the seven thunders sounded. ⁴And when the seven thunders had sounded, I was about to write, but I heard a voice from heaven saying, "Seal up what the seven thunders have said, and do*

not write it down." ⁵*Then the angel whom I saw standing on the sea and the land*
raised his right hand to heaven
⁶*and swore by him who lives forever and ever,*
who created heaven and what is in it, the earth and what is in it, and the sea and
what is in it: "There will be no more delay, ⁷*but in the days when the seventh*
angel is to blow his trumpet, the mystery of God will be fulfilled, as he
announced to his servants the prophets."

T he opening of the seventh seal leads to a profound silence in the heavenly court (8:1), perhaps a reference to Zephaniah 1:7, "Be silent
before the Lord God! For the day of the Lord is at hand." This dramatic pause quiets the constant worship of the angels and saints so that the
prayers of those suffering on earth may be heard in heaven. The prayers of the
early church are known from Scripture: "Come, Lord Jesus" and "Thy kingdom come on earth as it is in heaven." While the seven angels prepare to blow
the seven trumpets, "another angel" mediates the prayers of God's people and
presents them to God (8:3–4). The vision lets the worshipping church on
earth see its prayers from the side of heaven. The incense represents the
prayers of God's people ascending to God (Ps 141:2). As the incense ascends
before the heavenly throne, the persecuted community on earth recognizes its
own prayers. This reveals the earthly church participating in the worship of
heaven and forming one communion of the angels and saints with the
Christians in the world.

The prayers of the church are heard and release the power of God to act in
human history. The woes of the final days precede the coming of the Lord.
The burning coals of the censor are thrown upon the earth, causing lightning,
thunder, and earthquake, an expression of the mighty presence of God (8:5).
The coming of God's kingdom to the righteous is prepared by God's judgment of evil upon the earth.

Throughout the Bible, trumpets are blown to summon Israel to battle, to con-
vene worshippers for pilgrimage and solemn feasts, to install new kings, and to
call Israel to repentance and renewal. God's people associate sounding trumpets
with alarm, terror, praise, and joy. The seven angels sound the final climax of
God's triumph over evil and the coming of his kingdom (8:2, 6). With the seventh seal broken and the scroll laid fully open, the triumph of the Lamb is made
clear and the church's prayers for the coming of God's reign are answered.

Before the sounding of the seventh trumpet, "another mighty angel" came from heaven (10:1). The angel is described as a reflection of God and Christ, whose presence he mediates and whose message he delivers. His face "like the sun" recalls the opening vision of Christ (1:16). The rainbow mirrors the rainbow around God's heavenly throne (4:3). The "cloud" and "pillars of fire" suggests the guiding presence of God which led Israel through the wilderness of Exodus and who will bring his people to the kingdom.

The angel's vast size, bestriding the land and sea, with his right hand raised to heaven, brings together earth, seas, and sky. The message he bears is awesome and is sent from the Creator of "heaven and what is in it, the earth and what is in it, and the sea and what is in it" (10:2, 5–6).

The scroll held by the angel tells of the suffering and triumph of the church. Unlike the scroll with the seven seals, this scroll is already open (10:2). The angel announces that "there will be no more delay," and that "the mystery of God will be fulfilled" (10:7–8). God's purposes in creating the world will be completed, and the kingdom of the world will become the kingdom of God.

As seen from above, God's purposes are already fulfilled in the triumph of Christ. Sin and death are defeated and God reigns with Christ over heaven and earth. But seen from below, the church still struggles. The effects of Christ's victory are still unfolding in human experience. The ambiguity that results from living in God's reign that has already been established but is not yet fulfilled is difficult. We still need the angels as messengers, mediators, guardians, and guides until that day when all humanity will be one with the angels in giving glory and praise to God for eternity.

Reflection and discussion

• What is the purpose of the half hour of silence in heaven (8:1)? Why is quiet important to me in my relationship with God?

• In what way is the church's liturgy a participation in the eternal worship of God in heaven?

• What are the differences between the church as seen from above and from below? How do the visions of Revelation offer hope for the struggling church below?

• What aspect of the ministry of God's angels do I need the most? What have I learned about angels that is particularly helpful for me?

Prayer

Lord Jesus, the angels of heaven and the people of the earth bend their knees at your holy name. Extend your reign over all parts of my life so that all my words and actions will testify that you are Lord. May your kingdom come on earth as it is in heaven.

SUGGESTIONS FOR FACILITATORS, GROUP SESSION 6

1. Welcome group members and make any final announcements or requests.

2. You may want to pray this prayer as a group:

Lord God, all creation in heaven and on earth rightly gives you praise. Your people and your angels long for your final triumph over evil when you will bring your creation to its glorious completion. On that day your Son will come with all the angels as judge of all and gather us into your eternal kingdom. Then we will join with the angels and saints to adore your majesty and to rejoice in your presence forever. Send your Spirit upon us as we study your word and bless us with inspiration, generosity, and love for one another.

3. Ask one or more of the following questions:
   * How has this study of the angels helped your life in Christ?
   * In what way has this study challenged you the most?

4. Discuss lessons 25 through 30. Choose one or more of the questions for reflection and discussion from each lesson to discuss as a group.

5. Ask the group if they would like to study another in the Threshold Bible Study series. Discuss and select the topic and dates with those who are interested. Ask the group members to suggest people they would like to invite to participate in the next study series.

6. Ask the group to discuss the insights that stand out most from this study over the past six weeks.

7. Conclude by praying aloud the following prayer or another of your own choosing:

Holy Spirit of the living God, you inspired the writers of the Scriptures and you have guided our study during these weeks. Continue to deepen our love for the word of God in the holy Scriptures and draw us more deeply into the heart of Jesus. We thank you for the lives of your angels who serve as our mediators, messengers, guardians, and guides. Lead us to worship in more perfect harmony with the angels of heaven and bless us now and always with the fire of your love.

Ordering Additional Studies

To check availability and publication dates, or for a description of each study, visit our website at www.23rdpublications.com or call us at 1-800-321-0411.